I Used To Think I Was Normal, But Now I Take Pills For That

J.L. Black

ISBN: 1463762828
ISBN-13: 978-1463762827

LCCN:

DEDICATION

Scott and Kalin, the most important people in my life

&

My dearest Texas Trish and Funeral Home Amy,
the most *normal* people I know

CONTENTS

ACKNOWLEDGMENTS

These stories could not have been written without the comedic contribution - some of it on purpose - from the *normal* people in my life.

Much love and appreciation to:

Jessica Loucks, photographer extraordinaire! Not only is she an amazing photographer and artist, she is also the beautiful cover model!

John Badal, for his consultation, support, and expertise. More importantly, he is ultimately responsible (*at fault?*) for my twisted sense of humor.

Ann and George Wagner, for their encouragement and many, *many* hours spent reading and proofing. Ann continued to read my book long after I was sick of it. George is also the world's #1 Green Bay Packers fan!

My "Writers by the Bay" colleagues for their expertise and encouragement throughout this process.

1 WHAT THE HELL IS THIS BOOK ABOUT?

These stories are real, absolute, truthful pieces of fiction. I've exercised writer's liberty and I have told some accounts out of sequence so as to not completely give everything away, but for the most part these stories are true.

For you *normal* people reading this, let me clarify: when a person like me tells you something is true, by *true* I mean that after I've told myself something over and over and over again, before I know it, viola! it's true.

Set aside everything you think you know about being normal. Maybe there's no such thing. Maybe the only difference between normal people and people like me is the strength of the prescription pills we're popping.

2 I NEVER COMMITTED A MURDER BUT IF I DID

Just like O. J. Simpson, I was never convicted of murder. Unlike O.J. Simpson, I absolutely did it and I've got the gloves to prove it - and the gloves still fit.

Anyone who's ever been in a relationship knows they can be complicated for a number of reasons. Crazy ex-spouses, crazy current spouses, credit card debt, lack of money, too much money, children, religious differences, sexual preferences, and the in-laws are just a few complicating factors that I can name right off the top of my head. Eventually the honeymoon phase in every relationship ends and you wake up one morning many years later to the grim realization that you've spent the majority of your life, years you'll never get back, in this one relationship. You've given this person the best years of your existence - the years when you were young and full of hope and life, when you looked sexy in a bathing suit, and when people wanted to catch a glimpse of you naked. You've served your time and you'll be damned if you let your relationship end in divorce and let someone walk away with half your stuff.

I used to be horrified when I'd see stories on the news about spouses who murder one another, but after many years in a relationship of my own, I now appreciate why some married people consider murder a better alternative than separation or divorce. I'm not saying I condone or recommend murder and I certainly don't think committing murder is the answer to everyone's marital problems. All I'm saying is that after many years of being married, I now appreciate and understand the temptation.

I was only surprised to find out how quickly that temptation could set in with me and over what circumstances I would consider murder to be not only reasonable, but completely justifiable.

I am a dog person. I grew up with dogs, I understand dogs, and I love dogs. And the bigger the dog - Rottweiler, Newfoundland, Great Dane, Mastiff - the more I love them. As far as I'm concerned, any dog weighing less than seventy-five pounds is technically a *cat*. There's nothing better than coming home, even after a terrible day at work, and being greeted at the door by a dog. It doesn't matter if you've been gone for 8 hours or 15 minutes, a dog is genuinely excited to see you come home. The second you make it through the front door, a dog will bombard you with love and excitement.

Dogs love their people unconditionally. They are loyal and they can be the best friend or companion a person will ever have. You can tell a dog anything and everything and a dog will never give away your secrets. A dog won't talk about you behind your back, it won't have sex with your best friend, it won't judge you after you've polished off your 6th donut, and it won't care if you've outgrown all your fat clothes.

My newlywed husband turned out to be one of those *cat people*. He grew up with cats and he loves cats. And worse than that, this is something he never thought to bring up while we were dating. Instead, he decided to surprise me with this cat-loving secret 2 years into our married relationship. In fact, it was the day we were moving into our new apartment when my husband showed up at the front door with a bag of clothes and a pet carrier containing the biggest, hairiest, most feral-looking mess of a cat I had ever laid my eyes on. "Surprise! I thought he'd make a great housewarming gift!"

Oh, I was surprised alright. I stood in the doorway, mouth agape, as my brand new husband beamed at how his perfect housewarming gift had left me speechless.

Poison? Will he fit in the garbage disposal? Accidental overdose? Death by Pit Bull mauling? Unfortunate accident while cleaning a firearm? Smother to death with a pillow?

Fortunately for everyone involved, I was still experiencing that newly-wed blissful state in our relationship and the murderous thoughts left my head for the present moment.

How could I explain to my new husband that although I'd never owned a cat I just knew I hated them and I never wanted one in my house? What the hell was I supposed to do with a cat?

What are cats even for? I've never seen a cat owner out on a walk with their cat or playing fetch in the park. I've never even seen a cat respond to the sound of its name.

I have heard and read countless amazing stories about dog owners who were sick or unexpectedly died in their homes and their faithful dog continued to protect them. Some of these noble canines were so fierce in their loyalty and protection that they had to be shot with a tranquilizer and forced to relinquish their rightful place by their owner's side. Have you ever heard a story like that about a cat and their dead owner? Google it. There's no such story.

A cat at heart is nothing but a killing machine. It is pure predator. It will stalk and kill anything that moves. The second a cat owner starts looking like they could possibly be coming down with some sickness, a cat senses it and its whole demeanor changes. The previously detached and aloof cat suddenly becomes very concerned and interested about their owner's health and well-being. This is because the owner has now become *easy prey* as far as the cat is concerned.

Do you know what a cat does when their owner unexpectedly dies in their home? A cat will give their owner about a 1 day grace period to be dead - 2 days maximum - and then the cat will proceed to eat its owner's face. I repeat: the cat will proceed to eat its owner's face. True story. I saw it on an episode of "Sex and the City". A cat eating my face is all I think about every time I'm in some pet store on cat adoption day watching all the unsuspecting and soon-to-be faceless victims "ooohing" and "aaaahing" over the sweet little kitty cats.

I decided I would sound like a complete mental case if I tried to explain to my new husband that I lived in fear of a cat eating off my face, so I decided to give cat ownership a try for my marriage's sake. Maybe cat ownership wouldn't turn out to be as bad as I was dreading.

I bent down to get a closer look into the pet carrier and a pair of vapid, watery, half-closed eyes returned my stare. There's a popular saying that one should never underestimate their opponent, and I apparently forgot about that saying as I was assessing my enemy in the pet carrier. I mistakenly took the cat's impassive stare for dim-wittedness. I thought that poor wretched, retarded cat was too dense to pick up on the signals of hatred and disgust I was sending its way. I know now that it's not a matter of cats *not being able* to sense what others are feeling - they can absolutely sense what others are feeling. Cats just don't give a damn.

Cat litter. Multi-cat formula, extra strength, non-clumping, clumping, flushable, clay, corn-based, automatic cleaning sensors, bags on the bottom, illuminating crystals, natural recycled pellets - you name it, when it comes to cat litter, I've tried them all. And they all stink to high Heaven. I can't even sit through those ridiculous cat litter commercials anymore. The one I hate the most is the one where the cat calls in a bloodhound to help it locate its litter box. The advertiser claims that their cat litter is so fresh smelling, it's practically undetectable even to a bloodhound. Then the commercial ends with a bunch of little animated flower petals rising up from the litter box to make us think that the cat's shit smells just like spring flowers. Well I can tell you from first-hand experience that cat shit absolutely does not smell like spring flowers and I don't care what you sprinkle on top of it. In fact, cat shit doesn't smell like any flower I've ever smelled in my entire life, unless of course there's a flower out there that smells like cat shit. If there is, then it smells exactly like that one.

Because I cannot stomach the smell of a litter box, I was obsessive about keeping it clean. There is nothing that compares to the pungent ammonia-like stench of cat pee. If you've ever smelled it, you know exactly what I'm talking about. There's no mistaking it. You can smell cat pee the second you walk into a cat owner's home. One big whiff of cat pee is all it takes to get your eyes watering. My litter box cleaning routine consisted of me sitting half-crouched on the bathroom floor 2 times per day fishing for turds and other little balls of clumped treasure. I'd sit there with my face inches from the litter box, trying to breathe solely out of my mouth, afraid that the toxic acidity of the cat pee would singe off my eyebrows. There I'd sit, dragging that little rake through our clumping and flushable cat litter back and forth and back and forth. In some disgusting, twisted sense, I think I started to find the repetitiveness of the raking motion to be soothing, as if the litter box were my own little personal Japanese Zen garden.

Don't ask me when or how cleaning the cat litter became my sole responsibility in our household, but considering I never wanted a cat to begin with is a justifiable reason to commit murder if I've ever seen one. For you non-cat owners out there: congratulations, you lucky bastards for managing to make it this far in life without owning a cat, and although there are many, many cat litter products on the market that claim to be flushable, under no circumstances should you attempt to flush the entire litter box down your toilet at one time. Trust me.

Little by little, every aspect of cat ownership began to annoy and anger me. The disgusting litter box, the clawing-up of the little furniture we owned, and the cat's stand-offish attitude started to grate on my nerves. On a daily basis I'd come across massive clumps of cat hair throughout the apartment - stuck in between couch cushions, under the beds, and even stuck to the living room drapes. But even worse was coming across these clumps of hair on my bed and pillow. While I was at work during the day, that damn cat had obviously been making itself comfortable - no doubt just sitting there licking its ass - right on the pillow where I lay my face at night.

I started to hate this cat with a passion. Its stubborn refusal to come when I called it and its inability to act even slightly dog-like pushed me right to edge.

And then there were the hair balls.

The cat hair ball is perhaps the most foul and repulsive thing I have ever laid eyes on. Coming across a recently puked up cat hair ball is as shocking and horrifying as watching midget porn. It's as disturbing and disgusting as catching your seventy-something year old parents bent over, going at it doggy style. To be honest, I find midget porn to be more amusing and entertaining than horrifying, but it's still initially shocking and unexpected is all I'm saying.

So what is it about cat hair balls that makes them so revolting and sickening? Let me enlighten you...

Cats groom themselves by licking. As they lick themselves, they literally leave no stone unturned and no orifice unexplored. In the process, cats apparently lick off quite a bit of loose hair from their bodies, and the hairier the cat, the more hair they lick off and swallow. And the cat my husband brought into our lives was a big, fat, hairy mess of a cat. I know it may seem a little presumptuous of me to question God the Creator, but what was he thinking? If I were put in charge of creating a hairy animal that was supposed to groom itself by licking and I knew it was going to end up swallowing large amounts of its own hair, I think I would have created the animal with a stomach that could digest hair. I think the fact that God decided not to equip cats with a stomach that digests the hair they swallow proves that God is a dog person and simply hates cats.

As a cat grooms itself and swallows its own hair, the undigested hair that is left behind in the cat's stomach starts to gel with other bits and pieces of miscellaneous gunk they eat throughout the day - bugs, cat food, treats, birds, lizards - and all this miscellaneous gunk in the cat's stomach starts to form a big wad of gloop (I'm pretty sure that's the technical term veterinarians use for it). Oh, but we're not even at the gross part yet... the gross part occurs when this wad of gloop eventually makes its way out of the cat's stomach onto your living room floor or furniture. These semi-digested wads and clumps of hair, food particles, and other miscellaneous stomach contents are ejected from a cat's body via violent fits of coughing and hacking.

There is nothing quite like the sound of a cat preparing to eject a hair ball. Even if you've never experienced it, you'll know it's happening the second you hear it. This sound can't be confused with any other noise you've ever heard an animal make. This sound could wake me up from a dead sleep and would get me running around like the apartment was on fire. I'd run around in a panicked frenzy trying to locate the hacking cat, remove it from whatever piece of furniture it was standing on and throw it to the floor before it erupted.

The result of all this hacking and coughing is a big wad of gelatinous, bile-smelling, half-digested clumps of wet hair, sprinkled with little bits and chunks of multi-colored God-only knows-what. Cats deposit these gross hair balls on your carpet, your pillows, your couch, your kitchen table, or wherever it happens to be standing when it spontaneously becomes consumed by its hacking and retching. Coming across a recently puked up hair ball on your bedroom carpet is unquestionably gross. But what's grosser than gross? *Not finding it.* Until of course, you step in it with your bare feet as you run through the apartment in frantic search of the cat, only to discover you've found it 2 seconds too late.

Countless hair balls and hundreds of litter box changes later, I finally reached the point where nothing short of murder was going to make me happy. "That's absolutely it! That damn cat has just officially puked up its last hair ball on my carpet!" I vented to my close friend and neighbor, Nicole, who had heard my *I'm-so-sick-of-this-damn-cat* tirade at least one thousand times in the first month we owned it.

"So go drop it off at the animal shelter. Just say you let it out and it never came home."

"I'd love to! But then I'll have to spend days knocking on doors, putting up flyers, and pretending to look for it. I don't want to get into a huge fight over it, but I want this damn cat gone!"

Nicole is perhaps one of the most Internet-savvy people I know. Let's put it this way, I would never want to be the subject of an Internet investigation at the hands of Nicole. She is the master of all Internet trivia, weird news, and obscure facts. If it's out there, she knows it, or knows how to find it. And Nicole, perhaps not recognizing how dangerously perched I was on that little thin ledge that separates a normal state of mind from *wow, we better increase your medication* continued to share a little nugget of cat digestive system information with me:

According to *them*, a number of cats accidentally and tragically die each year as a result of a very common household product. *They say* one tablet of headache medication is all it takes. *Studies have shown* that a cat can't metabolize it. They go into complete renal failure. They swell up, vomit, have seizures, and die.

"Ok, I'll ask... how the Hell would you even know something like that?"

"The Internet."

Well *duh*.

A few days after my conversation with Nicole, I found myself standing at my kitchen counter looking out the window at my husband's cat as it was creeping around our back patio in search of the perfect place in my little flower bed to take a crap. I felt my left eye twitch as I watched the cat scratch and claw at the soil as it readied itself to deposit its special little gift to me. I adverted my eyes long enough to reconsider the bottle of extra-strength headache tablets I was holding, wondering if I had just finally and completely lost my mind. Was I really plotting to murder my husband's beloved pet? Was I seriously going to poison this cat? "You're damn straight I am!" I announced out loud to the empty apartment.

As I watched the cat pinch off the last of its turd and proceed to bury it where I would undoubtedly come across it the next time I was weeding the flowers, I popped open the bottle of the extra-strength headache medicine and shook out 3 tablets. I rationalized that if a tablet was all it took to kill a cat, then 3 tablets should make it a quick and painless death. Ok, everyone, please cut me some slack here. I'm really not a terrible person. I promise I'm not some crazy maniac running around the suburbs with a crossbow randomly murdering people's beloved pets. I just needed this one particular animal to be dead.

I started to grind and crush the tablets into a very fine powder and I was momentarily horrified when I caught myself humming and singing a few impromptu lines I had made up to the tune of "Camp Town Ladies":

Guess what kitty's gonna die today? Doo Da, Doo Da! Kitty's taken its last shit in my yard today, all the doo da day!"

Oh yeah, I had completely gone mental.

Once I was satisfied that the tablets had been ground into a fine enough powder so they would be imperceptible to the cat, I mixed it with half a can of un-drained tuna in oil. I thought the oil would sufficiently disguise the flavor of the medicine and would make it all go down smooth and fast. I figured it was important to have enough tuna in the mixture to completely mask the smell and taste of the tablets, but at the same time, I didn't want the lethal effect of the poison to be diluted.

Now that I was actually going through with the murder, there were many questions that started to nag at me: *Did the cat have to ingest the medicine on an empty stomach? What if the cat threw it up? How long will it take to die? Is it going to scream or make some weird noises as it dies? What if it dies right outside my apartment? Can you throw a dead cat out with the weekly garbage?*

I guess I should have spent a little more time researching the lethal tuna-to-headache medicine ratio for murdering a cat, but thanks to all the years I've spent watching " CSI: Crime Scene Investigation", I knew better than to do that kind of research from my home computer. There was no way I was going to leave behind that kind of forensic trail. Ok, maybe I watch a little too much television, but everything I see on "CSI" proves that it's always one little detail that screws up a perfectly good murder. I needed to pull off this murder on the first try and I didn't want to risk doing something careless that could later trace the murder back to me.

I wasn't certain if there was an animal homicide division assigned to the Northern Virginia police department, but I wasn't about to take any chances. I pinned back my hair and put on a pair of florescent pink dishwashing gloves to prevent me from leaving behind any trace samples of my DNA. I made sure to place the poisoned tuna mixture on a generic paper plate that can be purchased at any grocery store in the nation. I carried the mixture to the front door and took a quick look outside to make sure no one was around. A quick glance to my left and then a glance to my right, and it looked like the coast was all clear. I snuck out the front door carrying the plate in front of me as I called to the cat, "Heeeeere kitty kitty kitty... heeeere kitty kitty kitty..." After a few additional calls, the cat approached me meowing hungrily and it rubbed itself against my legs. I crouched down and placed the plate of tuna in front of the cat, coaxing it to eat.

"That's a nice kitty…. Are you hungry? You want some tuna? Here you go, I've made you a special tuna treat, you disgusting stupid hairy mess of a cat."

The cat cautiously approached the plate and sniffed the food. I couldn't believe how easy this was going to be! I caught my breath and held it in tense anticipation...

I then watched in disbelief as the damn cat turned its back to me and the plate of tuna and walked away. That damn cat walked away! It settled itself down into a comfortable position just a few feet from where I was standing and it proceeded to start licking its ass. And it was licking it quite thoroughly by the sounds I could hear. This stupid cat couldn't stomach the taste of tuna and yet it considered the taste of its own butt to be palatable? Do you understand now? This is *precisely* why this stupid, ridiculous cat needed to die.

I don't know how to describe the rage that consumed me at that particular moment as I sat watching the cat lick itself. I watched the cat continue to calmly lick itself for a few more seconds imagining that I would soon be seeing chunks of its butt in the next hair ball it deposited on my pillow. I think this was perhaps the moment I completely committed myself to seeing this murder through to the end.

I crept up to the cat on my knees, balancing the plate of tuna in one hand, all the while staring directly into its eyes, knowing this one shot was all I would get. *Do or die! Hoo-Rah!* The cat stopped licking itself as it passively watched my approach. It wasn't half as startled as I was when I reached out with one dishwashing gloved hand and grabbed it by the loose skin on the nape of its neck. I was amazed at how that maneuver caused the cat to go almost completely limp in my grasp as I jumped to my feet, dangling its limp body in mid-air.

I was holding the plate of poisoned tuna in my right hand and the cat in my left. Since both my hands were occupied, I didn't have much choice but to shove the paper plate directly into the cat's face, plastering it in tuna. This was not exactly turning out to be the calculated, clean murder I had envisioned. The moment the tuna made contact with the cat's face, it howled, shrieked, and clawed at me as it frantically tried to free itself from my grip. I was terrified, but still I refused to let go as the voices screamed inside my head: *The cat's going to eat your face! The cat's going to eat your face*!

I continued to hold the cat tightly with my arm completely extended away from my face as I persisted in smearing the cat with tuna, hoping some of it would miraculously make its way into its mouth as it howled and hissed. After I managed to smear most of the tuna onto the cat's head and face, I threw the cat to the ground and I jumped back, expecting that at any moment it would start throwing up or having convulsions. Instead, the cat hissed and spat at me, took a final swipe at my legs, and took off at a full sprint towards the back of the apartment complex.

I was terrified that the noise would attract the neighbors, so I took off running for the safety of my apartment. I locked the door behind me, pulled the shades closed and waited, crouched by the door, listening for the sound of approaching sirens from the animal homicide division. I spent the next hour sterilizing the crime scene and disposing of any incriminating evidence that could later be used to tie me to the murder. When I was done, I grabbed Nicole, we put on our dishwashing gloves and went canvassing the neighborhood, garbage bags in hand, in search of the recently deceased cat.

Ok, ok, everyone calm the hell down. Before some crazy vegan/vegetarian militant animal rights activist puts a contract out on me, let me assure you that no animal was harmed during this failed cat assassination. Please save your hate mail. Not only did the damn cat not die, it didn't even get sick. Sure, it walked around smelling like rotten tuna for about 2 days, but that was the worst of it. In fact, this stupid damn hairy fat cat ended up living with us for another 10 years until it finally passed away from old age. Yes, I've got the death certificate to prove it in case "CSI" comes knocking on my door.

Today, nearly 20 years into our married relationship, we are both a dog and cat household. I have my beautiful two-hundred pound Mastiff and my husband has his latest cat. And as much as I hate to admit it, I somewhat like this stupid damn cat. He's ok as far as cats go.

Our cat is a pure bred Siamese, but not the designer, genetically altered, pointy-faced skinny Siamese cats like the creepy twins on "Lady and the Tramp". Our cat is the traditional Siamese with the big round head and brilliant marble-like blue eyes. He lived with us for almost a week without a name as we argued about what we thought would be the best name for him. I still don't know why people even bother to name their cats. It's not like cats come when they're called. In fact, if you're not in immediate possession of something a cat wants, they don't even acknowledge your presence. Your job is simply to empty their litter box, feed them, and stay the hell out of their way.

My top choices for cat names were "Sonofastupidbitch" or "Damnit", since I figured that's what I'd be saying about it most of the time.

"Besides, don't you think that would be funny? The Veterinarian could call out to the waiting room for everyone to hear: *Sonofastupidbitch, we're ready for you!* or *Damn It, go into that exam room!*"

I was out voted and my son's choice for the cat name was chosen. So *Sumo* it is. As in *sumo wrestler*, which is quite appropriate as the cat is so fat it can barely reach around to lick its own butt. But that is absolutely one cat-owner responsibility I refuse to do. I'll continue to empty the litter, and my husband can take that one.

Sumo is a seal point Siamese, which means his body is primarily brown, but the points on the tip of his ears, tail, and his 4 paws are black. *He looks like he's wearing little bitty kitty boots and mittens,* I sometimes think to myself when I look at him. I have to admit that sometimes I look at Sumo and it makes a smile involuntarily form on my face.

But just as quickly, I can be overcome with a fierce impulse to kick Sumo right in his ass and send him skidding across our wood floors. I probably wouldn't kick him too hard, but just maybe hard enough to send him sprawling, with his cute little paws splayed, clawing frantically for traction.

And every once in a while as I sit watching Sumo groom and lick himself, I catch myself wondering if Sumo likes tuna.

3 CHUCK E. JESUS

They say you find certain things in your life at the time when you need it the most and when you least expect it. I think there might be some truth to that, but even so, I never expected to find Jesus in a Northern Virginia pizza parlor.

I was born, baptized, and raised in a strict Catholic household. If you're a practicing Catholic - or Catholic basher - you know that I, like most other Catholics, grew up with a laundry list of things God didn't want me wearing in public, things God didn't want me doing, things God didn't want me saying, food God didn't want me eating, and movies God didn't want me watching - and the list goes on and on and on...

Growing up in a strict Catholic household is like embarking on a wild Disney World rollercoaster adventure ride. Strap yourself in, keep your hands and feet inside the cart, and hang on tight! You're about to embark on a terrifying ride straight down into the fiery pits of Hell (which I guess is actually better than the crappy, anti-climatic gift shop finale). But I didn't just grow up Catholic. I grew up *Roman Catholic*. Roman Catholicism takes the standard vanilla Catholicism and raises it to the 10th power. It is the "X Games" of Catholicism. It's not for beginners or the faint of heart. Vatican headquarters should issue the Roman Catholic membership cards with a disclaimer:

Warning! May cause nausea, vomiting, dizziness, and irrational feelings of self-loathing. Many experience perpetual feelings of guilt. Other side effects may include spontaneous bouts of diarrhea, profuse sweating, and inexplicable fear of persecution and eternal damnation.

If you grew up in a Catholic household like mine, you know that attending church service - we call it mass - on Sundays was absolutely mandatory. In my home it was not only mandatory, but it was also mandatory to attend mass dressed in our Sunday best.

"Stop being ridiculous! God doesn't like girls wearing jeans and sneakers in His house!" is how my mother would explain it to me when I complained about the dress and tights she set out for me to wear.

My grandmother, an eighty-five year old Roman Catholic still covers her head in a black veil when she attends mass. I don't know why she does this and it's never occurred to me to ask. Catholic children aren't raised to ask questions. All I know is to this day, if I attend mass with my grandmother, I either cover my head with a handkerchief or else she'll slap a Kleenex or napkin or any other item she can find on top of my head prior to allowing me to enter God's house.

Another popular rule in Catholic households that bled into the school systems and some of our local restaurants is that no meat could be eaten on Fridays. Apparently there's a rule somewhere specifying that God doesn't want people to eat meat on Fridays. Again, it's never occurred to me to question it. For all I know this meat-free Friday rule may be clearly documented somewhere in the Bible, but as I've never read it, I can't argue it or quote the source. All I know is that no meat was eaten in our house on Fridays and no meat was served to us in our school cafeteria, either. Friday's menu in the Queen of Assumption Catholic School cafeteria was predictably "Fish Stick Friday". For whatever reason – I can't even pretend to understand it – fish does not fall under the meat category in the Catholic food pyramid. Neither does pepperoni. Our school menus on Friday were strictly reserved for Catholic non-meat items such as fish sticks and pepperoni pizza. I recommend you don't think about that too hard or else your head will literally explode.

One thing that Catholic-bashers out there may not realize is that although we survivors of our Catholic upbringing are fully aware that many of the rules we grew up with are crap, we are still helpless to do anything about it. All this Catholic crap was force-fed to us starting at a very young age and the rules were strictly enforced throughout our childhoods. Catholic children like me were not expected or encouraged to read the Bible and we were certainly not encouraged to presume we could conduct our own interpretation of what was written. In fact, many of us successfully graduated from Catholic schools without ever having laid our hands on a Bible.

As a Roman Catholic child I was taught that to question what we were told about the Bible was to question God Himself, or worse yet, my Roman Catholic mother. Do you know what happens to Roman Catholic children who are brazen enough to question why we are told to believe certain things or why we perform certain rituals? Their Roman Catholic martyr-of-a-mother laments, cries, and lectures for hours about *children obeying God's commandments and honoring their parents who are placed on this earth to enforce God's rules, and Mary, the Virgin mother who never had to suffer such ungrateful children, and Jesus hanging on the cross, blood oozing from his wounds, suffering and dying for our sins...*

So we grow up as Catholic children knowing to keep our mouths shut, heads down, and go through the motions. The object of the game is to make sure you get all the big ticket items checked off the Catholic to-do list before you die so you can go to Heaven. When you think about it, at the core, practicing Catholicism is a lot like playing a very simple children's board game. The object of the game is to move your soul to

Heaven. To get there, you simply follow the rules, perform a few rituals, and viola! you get to take the short cut through the conservatory straight to Heaven's gates. If you mess up along the way or stray off the designated path, you have to make a few stops at Confession. This will take your soul the long way around the game board, but you still end up in Heaven. It's really not that complicated and I don't understand why so many people out there enjoy bashing the Catholics. There are definitely worse things out there than being Catholic - terrorists, serial killers, and IRS auditors, for example.

But for whatever reason the public has chosen Catholicism to be the religion of choice to bash, and so it makes us the butt of many jokes: *what does a sexy Amish chick and a Catholic girl who likes anal intercourse have in common?* Answer: Neither one exists. There's no such thing. First off, there's no such thing as a sexy Amish chick. Secondly, you've got a better chance of meeting a 3-peckered billy goat in a Walmart parking lot before you'll meet a Catholic girl who'll take it up her poop-shoot sober and on purpose.

"How do you say such things? Who taught you this?" I can just hear my Catholic martyr-of-a-mother lamenting as she makes the sign of the cross and sprinkles holy water around herself in a circle of Roman Catholic immunity.

All I know is that it's been at least 20 years since I escaped my Roman Catholic compound, but if so much as a suppository finds its way into my ass I feel compelled to chant 10 Hail Mary's and get myself to confession. Something I have learned that I'd like to share with other Catholics out there in need of absolution as a result of some unintended anal mishap - do not under any circumstances dunk or wash your affected "dirty" body parts in the holy water vessel thing at the front of the Church. The Church really frowns upon that. Especially if you're not wearing the appropriate head cover.

I started attending Catholic school in Kindergarten and I attended all the way through high school. Part of the standard curriculum in private Catholic school was that we spent several hours each day in class dedicated to memorizing prayers and hearing Bible stories. Memorizing prayers was a very critical part of the curriculum at Queen of Assumption Elementary school. Students couldn't move on to the next grade level unless they memorized the assigned prayers and were able to regurgitate them back to the teacher.

Our teachers were mostly elderly female nuns - we had to address them as "sisters" - with wrinkles and weathered leathery necks. There's nothing more terrifying than an old, sexually frustrated nun. There was no way any of us was going to question anything those crazy old women said or did.

If we were caught speaking out of turn, passing notes, or looking like we were daydreaming, they would call us to the front of the class to publicly humiliate us. They would make us hold out our hands and they'd rap us hard on the knuckles or slap our palms with their rulers. Those rulers the nuns used on us back in the day weren't today's cheap plastic rulers that snap in 2 pieces upon impact. These rulers were the thick wooden ones with that small strip of metal that ran along the entire length of it. That metal strip could deliver one hell of a painful cut when the wood started to splinter and the metal started to separate from the ruler. The Queen of Assumption nuns would slap us with the rulers until our hands bruised and turned bright red or until we broke down and started crying.

If the hem on our Catholic uniform skirt was too short and our skirt rode above our knees, the nuns would smack us on the back of our legs with the ruler until our skin shone bright red to help us remember to ask our mothers to please alter the length. Some of these rulers must have been at least as old as the nuns themselves and were in rough shape from being abused throughout the years. I swear some of the rulers were stained light pink from the carnage. It's amazing none of us contracted Hepatitis.

One of the most hated and feared nuns in all of Queen of Assumption was an ancient nun we called "Sister Saliva". Sister Saliva earned her nickname shortly after we were assigned our seats in her 4th grade class and we discovered that she could spit for distance. She'd get so wrapped up in her holy rolling that she'd practically foam at the mouth. There'd be spittle flying in all directions as she ranted about some Catholic thing or another. This was very unfortunate for the students sitting in the first 2 rows who got to experience her overactive salivary gland first-hand.

Unfortunately for me sitting in the 5th row back, I learned that Sister Saliva also had a very keen sense of hearing for such an old crusty broad. And the 5th row in her classroom is where I was sitting the day she was lecturing us and she overheard me refer to her out loud to other students as "Sister Saliva". I just couldn't help myself. I was laughing so hard I had tears streaming down my face as I watched my fellow students in the first 2 rows attempt to subtly dodge her flying spit. I started cracking jokes, doing Sister Saliva imitations of her spraying the class with her spit, cracking to my class mates that we should be thankful that Jesus provided us with such an entertaining show.

> "This is better than the Sea World Shamu killer whale show! Hey, the audience at that show *pays* to get drenched. The Sister Saliva show is *free*!"

I was carrying on like such a non-Catholic fool that I never heard Sister Saliva bulling her way down the aisle coming straight for me, nostrils flared, spit flying, and ruler swinging. I do vaguely remember her grabbing me by my hair and yanking me from my seat, but I honestly don't remember much after that. I've either repressed it along with some of my other Catholic childhood trauma or I just suffer a blank spot in my memory as a result of the beating. Either way, in my book, Shamu the killer whale definitely had a better sense of humor than Sister Saliva ever did.

What happens next in the story is pretty predictable and cliché: girl grows up being force-fed Catholic crap and girl eventually rebels against everything she's ever been taught about religion. However, I never rebelled to the point of where I stopped believing in God - *just in case*. My inbred fear of God and burning in Hell is too deeply rooted. I just stopped believing that God cares if I attend church every Sunday in my Sunday best or if I eat meat on Fridays or what my preferred sexual position is. With everything else going on in the world I just can't believe that God would sentence me to the same Hell as murderers, rapists, and IRS auditors simply because I practice birth control. But then again, I've never read the Bible, so I could be completely wrong. Those could absolutely be *the rules* and I'm screwed. Satan may already have the best seat in the house reserved for me, front and center with a great view of the fireplace.

When I reached the point in my early 20's where I started seriously dating and making decisions about potential husbands, I decided that I had to make a clean break from the Roman Catholic compound once and for all, or risk being stuck in it forever. "An Episcopalian? What's an Episcopalian?" my mother asked when she found out I was seriously considering marrying the latest boyfriend.

"You can't get married in an Episcopal church. It won't count! Rome won't recognize your babies!" my mother continued to scream at me when she found out that I wasn't even planning on getting married in a Catholic Church.

Just between you and me, I wasn't really against getting married in a Catholic Church, but the fact that it was driving my Catholic martyr-of-a-mother bat-shit crazy was just an unexpected bonus for me.

My first choice for places to be married was actually the very romantic and beautiful Saint Mary's Catholic Church. I made the mistake of thinking that I could just walk in, present my membership card, and make a reservation. The reality was we first had to contact Saint Mary's corporate office and schedule an appointment for an initial screening with their marriage coordinator, Sister Agnes.

Our screening with Sister Agnes started off pleasantly enough with a quick tour of the church and easy questions like how long my fiancé and I had known each other and why we wanted to get married. Then the gloves came off and it got super-Catholic super-fast.

"Are you both Catholic and active members of this parish?"

"Um, ok, sure. Why do you ask? I mean, yes, of course we're both Catholic, that's why we're here in a Catholic Church. To be married as Catholics."

"There is a required pre-marital counseling retreat for all couples wanting to be married. With you both being Catholic, a 3 weekend retreat is all you'll need to complete. After you complete the retreat, Father Brody will conduct your 2nd interview and schedule you for your premarital counseling sessions. Once you've completed that, we can discuss the wedding date."

"Any chance we can speed that up? We've already set the wedding date and we need to be married next month."

Sister Agnes raised her eyebrow as I continued to blurt out and babble nervously.

"Oh, no, it's not like *that*. I'm not pregnant or anything, it's just that we're ready to send out the invitations."

"I'm sorry, that's just out of the question. It can take several weeks alone to receive the records from Rome."

"Records? Rome keeps records?"

"Yes, your baptism records. You told me you are both Catholic. We need the records from Rome to confirm this."

I felt a cold bead of sweat start to form on my upper lip and I started having Sister Saliva flash backs.

"Wow, so Rome really keeps baptism records, huh? On *every single* Catholic? Ok, hypothetically speaking, what if for some reason Rome found my records but couldn't find my fiancés? What if they lost his record? Can we just send Rome some money? I think I brought my checkbook..."

At this, Sister Agnes wrinkled her nose as if she just caught a whiff of a very offensive odor.

"Rome doesn't lose records. Exactly what is going on here young lady?"

This is the point where my Episcopal-heathen fiancé came to my rescue, grabbed me by the arm and led me quickly out the door as he politely thanked Sister Agnes for her time. I let myself be pulled along, stumbling behind him, trying to keep a calm façade while the voices inside my head screamed out in a panic: *Oh my God, I just lied. Oh my God, I just lied to a nun! I just lied to one of God's nuns while I was sitting in His House!*

"Well, well, well", joked my fiancé when we were back in the car with the air conditioning blasting straight in my face to keep me from passing out.

"If lying to a nun while sitting in a Church and trying to bribe the Pope in Rome doesn't get you a one-way express ticket to Hell, I don't know what will."

Obviously we didn't get married at St. Mary's Catholic Church. To my mother's dismay, we ended up being married in an Episcopal Church by a reformed ex-Catholic priest who was himself divorced, re-married, and recently back from his honeymoon. Hey, we were working against a short deadline. It was either that or go with a Universal Utilitarian ceremony and be married by a lesbian lay-minister dressed in a toga and sandals. I don't think my mother would have survived that.

For some inexplicable reason, 6 years into our marriage after I gave birth to our son, religion suddenly became a very important topic to me and the main cause for much heated discussion in our home. I admit I may have suffered from a little post baby-delivery hormonal craziness, but for the most part I think I was feeling extreme Catholic anxiety about not having baptized my son as soon as he was born. Baptism is one of the *big* Catholic rituals, even for a fallen semi-recovered Catholic like me. It is one of the big ticket items that you absolutely have to get checked off the Catholic to-do checklist or you risk your soul's eternal damnation.

According to Catholic folklore, any child who dies before the age of 8 and has not been baptized gets a free pass into Heaven, but after the 8 year cut-off mark, a person is either baptized or they burn in Hell. Period. Game over.

The ritual of Baptism also appears on my husband's Episcopal checklist, but apparently they've got an open-ended due date, so my husband wasn't feeling the same panicked urgency I was feeling. The arguments in our household started when my very reasonable Episcopal husband mistakenly thought he could logically argue with me and de-program some of the damage the Catholic virus had done to my brain.

> "Think about it. Why is 8 years old the cut off age? Why is there a due date for when a person is baptized? The Baptists don't even baptize their children until they turn 16 so they can understand what being baptized means."

My husband's point certainly made sense to me on a logical, cerebral level, but let's face it, that's not where superstition and childhood trauma reside. I opened my mouth intending to present some brilliant counter-point that would make my husband understand my perspective, but instead, out spewed the poison from my Catholic childhood brainwashing.

"I really don't care what the freaking Baptists do!" I shrieked in a pitch high enough to attract the attention of the neighbor's dog.

Then I burst into a torrent of hysterical post-partum sobbing. I had hot tears and snot rolling down my face as I continued to scream at my husband in my Roman Catholic panic-induced sermon.

"My child has to be baptized now! If he dies without being baptized, God won't let him into Heaven with me. While you're just standing here talking to me about Baptists my son's getting closer to burning in Hell!"

Sister Saliva would have been so proud of me.

Although Prozac isn't technically recognized as an organized religious following (yet), through it, I, like many of its other devout followers, was able to minimize some of my Catholic-induced anxieties. The subject of baptism got put on the back burner for the time being and we agreed to start off on our quest for the appropriate place to baptize our child by visiting some of our local churches and find one we were both comfortable with. That sounded like a very rational, sensible, Episcopal approach, but just like with any plan, sometimes the unexpected happens along the way and you are forced to resort to plan B.

We did eventually end up getting our son baptized, but it wasn't until he turned 5 years old, which for the record, still falls within the mandated Catholic cut-off date. But my son's baptism didn't come as a result of any persuasive or hysterical arguments or us having found the perfect church, either. In fact, we were still working on our tour of the local churches when we unexpectedly found Jesus in a Northern Virginia pizza parlor called Chuck E. Cheese's.

Like many other children his age, our child was a huge fan of the Chuck E. Cheese's pizza parlor and the Chuck E. Cheese's birthday party experience. In case you haven't had the privilege, Chuck E. Cheese's is a huge franchise warehouse-size pizza parlor and arcade establishment that also rents out party rooms. It doesn't get any easier than hosting a birthday party at Chuck E. Cheese's. The parents just show up, write a check, and Chuck E. Cheese's handles the rest. The pizza they serve is typical and greasy and barely deserves the accolade of "edible" as far as I'm concerned, but the pizza is not what draws the children.

Flashing lights, loud music, hundreds of arcade games, skeet ball machines, prizes, and numerous climbing contraptions are just some of the attractions, most of which require the parents to fork over/exchange cash for game tokens. Thankfully there is a very conveniently located ATM and *Exchange Your Cash for Tokens!* machine found every 3 feet within the pizza parlor.

The climax of the Chuck E. Cheese's birthday party experience occurs when Chuck E. Cheese himself, resplendent in his mouse suit regalia, graces the crowd with his majestic mouse presence. And the kids go wild, folks! The entire pizza parlor erupts into seizure-inducing flashing strobe lights and deafening music to broadcast Chuck E. Cheese's arrival. A throng of hundreds of children start to convulse wildly and they scream at the top of their little lungs as they follow Chuck E. Cheese around the pizza parlor. They form a massive conga line, they sing happy birthday to the lucky Chuck E. Cheese birthday child, and they chant in unison to their idol: "Chuck...Eeeee! Chuck...Eeeee! Chuck Eeeee!"

Our particular pizza parlor in Northern Virginia also serves pitchers of beer for the unfortunate adults who find themselves trapped within its walls for hours. I don't know which Senior Vice President at the Chuck E. Cheese's corporate headquarters came up with the idea of serving alcoholic beverages in this establishment, but he's a freaking genius as far as I'm concerned. Now all they need are some vending machines that dispense ear plugs and extra-strength headache pills and I can almost stomach the Chuck E. Cheese's birthday party experience without feeling like I want to stick a gun in my mouth.

Several Chuck E. Cheese's birthdays parties later and a few weeks before the Christmas holidays, I was setting up my nativity set in front of our fireplace with my 5 year old son. His job was apparently to teach me patience as he painstakingly unwrapped figurines in super-slow motion before handing them to me. With every figure he handed me I would attempt to impart my very fragmented and almost fictional knowledge of the story of Jesus' birth. I held up each figure and attempted to explain to my son their religious significance. I would say things like, "This is one of the wise men who followed the star to find baby Jesus" or "This is a camel that carried the wise men". And my son would regurgitate back to me, "That's a wise man who followed the star" or "That's the camel".

As is customary in my house, the last figures to be placed in the manger are Mary, Joseph, and the baby Jesus. When I held up the figure of baby Jesus, I got a little emotional and I could feel my Catholic roots taking a strangle hold on me. I had no choice but to break into full sermon:

> "This is the baby Jesus. Christmas is not about Santa, or reindeers, or toys. Christmas is about baby Jesus and his birthday. Christmas is a birthday party for baby Jesus."

At the mention of the birthday party I saw my 5 year old's little face light up with pure religious rapture as his brain made the connection. He asked me, "Chuck E. Jesus?" And before I could correct him, he immediately started to cheer at the top of his lungs:

> "Chuck E. Jesus! Chuck... Eeeee!! Chuck... Eeeee! Chuck... Eeeee!"

I was horrified and frightened that God was going to send down a bolt of lightning and kill us where we stood. I made the sign of the cross and frantically tore apart our kitchen junk drawer in search of anything that could possibly pass as a rosary that I could chant over. I screamed to my husband who was sitting in the next room, "Oh Sweet Mary Mother of God! Oh Sweet Whistling Baby Jesus! Did you hear what your son - did you hear what your *un-baptized* son - just said in front of Mary and the baby Jesus?"

Of course my husband had heard it, but the heathen was laughing too damn hard to be of any help whatsoever. "This is *not* funny!" I screamed and spat in my Sister Saliva voice.

"Go find a baptism joint! Drive through, 24-hour place, I don't care! Find a place and tell them we need our son baptized immediately - it's an emergency!"

For the record, if anyone asks me, I'm Roman Catholic. Granted, I'm probably not what Vatican headquarters would consider to be an exemplary card holder. I don't go to mass every Sunday, and in my house we eat meat on Fridays. I use birth control, I curse (both in written and oral format), and I sometimes take the Lord's name in vain.

But active card holder or not, on any of the mandatory Catholic mass days like Easter Sunday or Christmas, you better believe you'll find me sitting in a Church pew wearing my Sunday best, with my head appropriately covered.

Just in case.

4 PAIN IS TEMPORARY. PRIDE IS FOREVER!

I am a soccer family survivor. I am a survivor of an uber-competitive soccer family childhood. My dad and uncle both played soccer their entire childhoods. As adults they played soccer at the semi-professional level and then in their spare time, when they weren't watching soccer on TV, they were coaching kids' soccer teams. This meant that all the kids in our family played soccer for at least a season or 2, whether they liked it or not. Fortunately for me, it was quickly discovered that I had no athletic ability or coordination, and I completely lacked a competitive spirit, so my soccer career ended 3 weeks into my first season when my dad cut me from his team. Hey, it's soccer, it's not personal.

Because the cycle of soccer abuse is hard to break, when my son turned 6 years old I was determined that he too, would play soccer. I dove head first into my role of soccer mom for his pee-wee team, the adorable little Blue Blazers. The Blue Blazers were just the sweetest little team of munchkins! They were so cute with their little blue shirts and their little blue shorts and their little blue shin pads and their little blue socks! And the Blue Blazers *sucked*. Out loud. The Blue Blazers couldn't have won a soccer match against kids playing with no legs. We did end up winning 1 game that season, but that was due to the other team having to forfeit as 4 of their players were on quarantine for chicken pox.

Practice after practice I would sit quietly at the sidelines with the other soccer moms, all of us pretty much cut from the same stereotypical soccer mom template: Starbucks coffee in one hand, reading material in the other. We'd sit at the sidelines compiling our grocery lists, addressing invitations, and stuffing envelopes for some school event or fundraiser. We would chat with each other about the kind of day we had, parties we were planning or attending, school activities, and we'd even swap recipes. We did not sit on the sidelines and talk about the Blue

Blazer team statistics or our kids' soccer skills (or more realistically, their lack thereof), and we certainly did not coach our children from the sidelines. In fact, I think the most animated display of emotion I ever heard on a pee-wee soccer sideline was the sound of polite clapping when one of the teams scored, which didn't happen very frequently. The rowdiest remark I'd ever heard from a disappointed parent on a pee-wee soccer sideline was "That's ok, try harder next time!"

Game after game I watched my 6 year old and the adorable Blue Blazers lose. The end of season statistics for the Blue Blazers reflected: 1 win 9 losses 0 ties. But in no way did that prevent the soccer moms from throwing the team an end-of-season celebration to rival the World Cup festivities. We rented a party room resplendent with blue balloons, streamers, and banners. We had Blue Blazer cupcakes with blue sprinkles, a huge soccer sheet cake decorated with little soccer player figurines and soccer balls. There were cookies, moon bounces, and a clown making blue balloon figurines for the kids. Each player was presented with a "Good Effort!" medal that the coach proudly hung around their necks as if they were Olympians. He praised each player for their hard work and good sportsmanship throughout the season and told them to sign up again for the following year.

A few years later my quiet, polite, soccer world came crashing down around me as my husband and my 9 year old son informed me that football was the sport they wanted to play. I remember standing helplessly at my husband's side in absolute shock, mouth agape, as I took in the mobile football recruiting post that had been planted in the middle of the elementary school recess yard. I remember feeling short of breath, choking back tears, as I took in the huge gray recruiting and processing pavilions which made the elementary recess yard look like an Army M.A.S.H. unit. There were men and women screaming directions through bull horns, shoving forms into our hands, coaches blowing whistles and directing boys and their parents to quickly process through each station based on their age and weight. It was mass, organized chaos. I didn't know what was happening, but whatever it was, it was happening quickly.

We were herded with a group of other boys my son's age into the first pavilion where my 9 year old was asked to remove his shoes and step on a scale. "All right! Way to go, momma! Whatcha feeding this one?" The weigher then turned to scream at one of the coaches, "Hey, coach, we've got ourselves a *big* one here!" Before I could react, I noticed a little freckled-face 6 year old boy rush past me. He was signing up for the "ankle-biter" football division for children weighing under sixty-five pounds. He had a shaved head and I think he may have been sporting some tattoos, but he was moving too fast for me to be positive. But I can tell you for certain that he was wearing his recently issued football camp T-shirt proclaiming "Pain is Temporary. Pride is Forever!" I felt my anus clench as I read those words on his shirt. And I mean it clenched tight. Roman Catholic tight.

"Oh my God, what the Hell are we signing our son up for? These are *maniacs*. Did you see that little boy with the shaved head and that insane T-shirt?"

"Shhhh. Don't embarrass your son. One of these guys is going to be his coach."

I spent the rest of the morning choking back the vomit that kept threatening to erupt as I followed a few steps behind my son and excited husband as they hurried from tent to tent.

"My son is going to play football just like me and his Grandpa!"

I watched in dread as my sweet little boy was fitted with more battle gear than a war elephant prepared for combat: ridiculously over-sized shoulder pads that I haven't seen since the 1980's, mouth guard, chin strap, thigh pads, knee pads, side pads, back pads, butt pads… and we still had a list of items of a more personal nature to pick up at a sporting goods store later on that evening. Once completely outfitted in his football gear, my son looked ridiculous. He looked like a human "bobble head", hardly able to keep his head balanced under all the added weight. But my little boy beamed up at me with a huge smile on his face and I momentarily felt a little better. After all, under all that protective gear, what's the worst that could happen?

Have you ever experienced one of those "Dorothy, you aren't in Kansas anymore" moments? Mine occurred the minute I was formally introduced to a species of our populace that I had heard about and I'd seen on TV but had never encountered in person: the "football parent", better known as *parentus fanaticus maximus*. Within seconds I could tell that the parental experience on a football sideline was going to be nothing like a soccer mom sideline. Anyone remember doing analogies on the Standard Aptitude Tests in school?

Football is to Soccer as:

a. Thrash metal mosh-pit is to Josh Groban
b. Thrash metal mosh-pit is to Ballet
c. Thrash metal mosh-pit is to Opera

The correct response is: d). All of the above. And then some.

I discovered that the football sidelines are full of loud, aggressive people who are passionately engrossed in every play of the game. They scream out directions and criticisms to all kids on the field. They aren't shy about voicing their opinions about their kids, other people's kids, the coach, or the referee. They also use very aggressive and non-soccer sounding words like Hit him! Drive it! Run him down! Bring it! Fire it up! Lock and Load! Take him down!

And these are the *women*.

I was horrified. I felt completely lost and out of my soccer-mom element, and I was scared for my son's life.

Day one of my son's football combine camp I showed up looking completely out of place with my reading material in one hand and my non-fat, half-soy, extra-hot caramel latte in the other. Within 5 seconds one of the real football moms spotted me and offered to help me find my way to the nearest soccer field.

I watched in mortified fear as my son ran out to join the rest of his team to the sound of whistles blowing and coaches screaming at everyone to *hustle!* and *fire it up!* I stood on the sidelines in mute terror next to a woman bellowing at a fallen child.

> "Shake it off! It aint broken! Get up and do your damn job!"

I followed her intense gaze to her 10 year old who was stuck on his back. The poor kid was rocking from side to side as he struggled against the forces of gravity and the weight of the huge football helmet that kept pulling him into reverse and onto his back like some pathetic overturned turtle. My immediate instinct as a virgin football mom was to run onto the field to make sure the boy wasn't hurt. I wanted to help him up, maybe swab him with a little antibiotic and walk him to my car to get a cookie. To my surprise, no football mom moved from the sideline to help the boy as he struggled to right himself. Instead, other moms joined his mother in encouraging him.

"Shake it off! Get up! Go hit him back!"

And sure enough he did. Within a few seconds he righted himself and proceeded to quickly demonstrate the popular saying "payback is a bitch" as he tackled the player who had apparently flattened him first.

I cringed, winced, and covered my ears at the sounds of the pads and helmets crashing against each other. However, for whatever reason, the sound of crashing football gear sent the other moms into an intense cheering frenzy. They went wild, giving each other high five's, seemingly completely unconcerned about the possibility of their children being permanently disfigured or mutilated. Within the next few hours of drills I watched my son get plowed, tackled, dragged, and dog piled. I sat mutely on the sidelines with my eyes welling with hot tears as the coaches yelled non-stop at the kids to move faster, stay lower, and hit harder. The other moms were completely unsympathetic to my fear and discomfort and were brutal with their cheering as they goaded the boys to hit each other harder. By the end of the practice session I was ready to grab my son off the football field and never look back.

The first full week of football practice was just as brutal and bloody off the field as my husband and I battled it out at home. My husband accused me of being too soft and of attempting to baby our son indefinitely and I accused my husband of trying to relive his football glory through our son. I screamed that our son was going to suffer some injury that was going to make him retarded and incapable of giving me grandchildren some day.

"What's the point of having him wear all this damn stuff if it doesn't even protect him?"

I would cry as I as helped extricate my son from his football gear to find new bruises developing over old, half-healed purple splotches and welts. I cried, threatened divorce, and secretly plotted to poison or smother my husband to death with his pillow as he slept.

"Do you even know what that insane coach was saying to the kids tonight? *Hit them hard*! *Lock and Load*! *Run through them*! *Bring the train*! Bring the train? What the hell is that? I don't even know what that means!"

I blubbered and sniveled as my husband patiently explained to me again for the hundredth time how important it was for a boy to play sports and be part of a team.

"He should stick it out at least 1 full season to see if he likes it. Besides, we've already spent hundreds of dollars on football camp, uniform, and pads."

"I don't give a flying rat's ass how much money we've spent! I promise you it'll be less than brain surgery and physical therapy!"

After a few more days of heated arguing, my husband and I decided to call a truce. We recognized that having me on a football field sideline was about as valuable and useful as a nice set of 38DD tits on a nun. We agreed that I would not attend any practices for a few weeks until my son got better and learned to take a hit without getting hurt. I agreed to let the boys do their "football thing" and in exchange, they agreed to tell me absolutely nothing about what was going on. All I wanted was to survive this 1 season of football through a blissful state of absolute ignorance. Our version of the military's "don't ask, don't tell" agreement seemed to be working out pretty well for us – at least until week 3 into my son's football career when my husband brought my son home to me bleeding and wounded.

My sweet little boy was bloodied, bruised, and cut. Both of his elbows were ripped up, he had a gash on his right knee, he had blood trickling down both his legs, and his right sock was stained pink from where he'd apparently been bleeding for a little while. His hair was plastered with sweat, he had dirt caked all over his face and he was limping. Undoubtedly my husband had debriefed him on the ride home because I could tell my boy was doing his best not to cry in front of me.

"Oh my God, what the hell happened? Baby, come here! Oh baby, oh baby, come here and let momma take a look at you!"

My husband, who was putting away the football gear called back to me from the laundry room,

"Just relaaaax and leave him alone. He's fiiiiine. They were just doing some contact drills today and he got dragged through the rocks a little."

"My shoulder hurts, too, mom."

"Your shoulder? Why the hell does his shoulder hurt? What the hell happened to his shoulder?"

"Nothing. He's fiiiine... it was hot, so they weren't wearing their complete set of pads today and a kid speared him in the shoulder with his helmet."

I felt my eye twitch as I turned against my husband in a fit of frustrated rage.

"They weren't wearing their pads? You mean the freaking pads we spent hundreds of dollars on to protect his body from permanent injury? Are those the pads you're talking about? These maniacs are going to do permanent damage! My son will end up sterile and retarded and he'll be living at home with us forever and then I guess you'll finally admit that he shouldn't be playing football!"

I turned back to my son who had now started to openly cry, mostly because I think I was scaring the hell out him.

"Oh my God! Did the coach examine your shoulder? Can you move your shoulder, honey? Did they put ice on it? Does your shoulder feel like it's going to pop out of its place like it's dislocated?"

"Oh for Christ sakes, calm down, you're scaring the crap out of the kid. It's football! Things like this are going to happen. He's fine. Shake it off, big guy – go jump in the shower and you'll feel better."

I shot my husband a parting filthy look as my son stepped into the shower and I went running to gather first aid supplies. Antibiotic, children's pain reliever, bandages, ace wrap, icy hot, 2 cold compresses, half a glass of warm milk, and 4 chocolate chip cookies later and I was slowly starting to feel a little bit better and was able to regain my indoor soccer-mommy voice.

"Honey, are you sure you're ok?" I whispered to my son as we lay next to each other in his bed, me trying not to touch any of his sore spots and him trying not to smear antibiotic all over his football-themed bed sheets.

"I'm fine, mom. I'll be ok tomorrow," he replied.

"I'm so proud of you for sticking with this. Will you honestly tell me something, though? Do you really like football? Do you *really* want to play football?"

And that's when my sweet little child innocently drove the nail into my husband's coffin, "Well, football wasn't exactly my idea, you know. Dad really wanted me to play."

Watching my little boy get abused and manhandled like some tackle dummy, the coaches screaming incessantly like Army drill sergeants, the insanely competitive football parents – none of these things prepared me for what was to happen next. To this day I'm not certain I understand it myself.

The last Saturday in September we played a game against a rival city football team called the

Colts. A few minutes into the first quarter of the game my son, the offensive tackle, was lined up against a Neanderthal of a kid who I feared was going to smash him to pieces right in front of my eyes.

> "Oh please! Someone gimme a flipping break! There's no way in hell that kid out there is only 11 years old! Come on, Ref, he's got a 5 o'clock shadow I can see from here for Chrissakes!"

> "Just please be quiet..." my husband warned as we watched my son and the Neanderthal face off across from each other.

The referee blew the whistle signaling the start of the play and through my half-hidden eyes I watched my son and the Neanderthal take a running start towards each other. I recall hearing a loud crashing sound as the Neanderthal and my son's body made contact as I stood on the sidelines chanting, "please don't retard him... please don't retard him... please don't retard him..."

When my son and the Neanderthal collided, I could feel the impact from where I stood cowering behind my hands, diarrhea threatening to spew from my body at any second. No one was more surprised or relieved than I was to look up and see my son still standing on his feet. "Whoa! What a Moose!" joked one of our football moms as she congratulated me by slapping me hard on the back.

It took a few seconds for what had happened to fully register in my mind, but when it did, I physically felt something inside of me snap. I felt a surge, an instant jolt of electricity course through my body. It was a raw, brutal, primitive, sensation that made me feel hot from the inside out - and then I felt it start to spread.

My sweet little boy had plowed into that Neanderthal of a kid and had thrown him off his feet and sent him crashing to the ground! My son had hit him with such force that the Neanderthal had landed flat on his back and wasn't moving. Let me reiterate: flat on his back. Sweet Jesus forgive me, but I'm pretty certain that specific moment was the closest I will ever come to having a true religious experience.

In my religious rapture, I almost knocked over a pregnant woman and some God awful ass-ugly kid in a stroller so I could bull my way closer to the sidelines to scream out my victory cry, "Oh, yeah, baby! That's what I'm talking about! That's my boy! Now we're playing some football!"

I don't know if this is the same type of experience for a guy watching his favorite football team slaughter their rival, but wow, what a panty-melter! I think I orgasmed.

I didn't know what was happening to me, but every game going forward I showed up at the field more excited about football – I even started to learn some of the rules. I came to the games wearing our team jersey and MVP pin with my son's number on it. I wore football beaded necklaces and head bands with boinging football antennas and I had my finger and toenails painted to match the team colors. I came to the games armed with whistles, mega phones, cow bells, clappers, and air horns. I talked some of the other parents into painting their faces the team colors, but they drew the line at shaving players' numbers in their heads, thinking that may have been a little overboard.

I became completely obsessed by the game. Maybe I was just letting go of all the pent-up soccer frustration from having watched my son and the Blue Blazers lose game after game. These kids definitely weren't the Blue Blazers – my son's football team was good! We were winning! I think my behavior was starting to worry my husband a little, but he knew better than to say anything – after all, it was him who brought this into our house to begin with.

My husband would sit on the sidelines with me, cheering for our son, and would do his best to diffuse my growing sideline aggression. But there was no stopping this train. I was a football mom possessed. I was in it to win it one-hundred-and-fifty percent. I'd grab my husband by the shirt and command him, "You get in there and tell that son of yours if he doesn't hit someone and hit someone hard right now we are cancelling Christmas!" Sometimes I'd turn my enthusiasm for the game onto the football field and scream directly at my son. "Look at me! You see this face? This is not a happy face! Get in there and hit someone and hit them hard!"

Game after game I could feel the football demon inside me growing. It was festering as it threatened to take complete possession of my body until the 1 game when it finally happened. The game we played against the undefeated Mustangs marked the moment my football demon completely broke free and took over. I'll call my demon "Cybil" to make it easier for you to tell us apart. Now I don't know if Cybil is what my football demon calls herself, but I do know one thing for certain: Cybil aint Catholic.

Cybil completely outdid even the most fanatic football parent and crossed that line to the point where she would never again be welcome into the polite society of soccer moms. Now before I get too far into this story, I want to point out that sometimes things sound a lot worse than they actually are when they are said out loud. Case in point, try saying this: "Yesterday I got into a full blown knock-down brawl with a crippled guy in a wheelchair and I kicked his ass! I mean, I beat that crippled guy to the ground!"

Granted, that doesn't sound too awful in your *head*, but the second you verbalize it out loud to other people, it sounds a little harsh. And the people will judge you. Trust me. Now admittedly, from where I sit today, Cybil's actions may have been a little much, but during a high stakes football game with all the testosterone and adrenaline pumping, sabotaging a guy in a wheelchair just seemed like the right thing for Cybil to do.

The wheelchair-bound coach for a football team called the Ravens showed up at our game against the Mustangs to spy on us before we played his team the following weekend. When I recount the story to you it may come off sounding like I'm a horrible person to be bullying the physically disabled, but I assure you, he absolutely had it coming.

Had the Ravens coach/spy given his reconnaissance mission a little more foresight, neither I nor Cybil may have noticed him at all. However, he stuck out like a sore thumb for several reasons. For starters, he was the only person on our side of the field not cheering or wearing our team colors. In fact, he was wearing a dark purple shirt blatantly advertising his affiliation with the Ravens. What made him even more obvious was that he would also periodically stop to jot a comment down on a small pad of paper after a major play.

He was also the only individual at the football game attempting to navigate the soggy sidelines in a wheelchair. He wasn't in just any wheelchair, either. He was sporting one of those tricked-out, light-weight racing models with the off-road tires. And from the skill in which he was evading the water puddles it was pretty obvious he was a skilled wheelchair operator. So don't let the wheelchair distract you, folks - think of the children! The children are the real victims in this story and Cybil was going to be damned if she sat back and let that man victimize her children - not to mention screw up their chance at making the play offs.

"Are you kidding me?" I exclaimed to our offensive line coach on the sidelines. "Is that really the Ravens coach out here scouting us out before our game against him?"

"Yeah. The Ravens do that a lot. At least this time he's not video-taping. Maybe you and some of the moms can subtly stand in front of him and block his view?"

And here's where I verbalized out loud, "Sure, coach, I'll try to get some of the moms together", but Cybil screamed inside my head *Lock and Load! Bring the train!*

I rounded up 3 other football moms and told them what was going on.

"You want us to roll him?" asked the Quarterback's mom.

"No! We are absolutely not rolling a crippled guy in a wheelchair," I hissed at her, all the while Cybil was thinking *I knew there was something I liked about this woman!*

We agreed to form a wall of football moms in front of the coach so he couldn't see the plays from where he sat in his wheelchair. We snickered and giggled like school kids as we put our dastardly plan into action. When the coach rolled his wheelchair 2 feet to the left to get out from behind us, we moved 2 feet to the left to re-obstruct his view. We planted small children in his path, repositioned water coolers to block his route and when he rolled his wheelchair 2 feet to the right, we moved our group 2 feet to the right. This crazy Texas two-step routine was ridiculous and it seemed like the coach could play this game as long as we could. *Roll 2 steps to the left! Take 2 steps to the right! Do-si-do and we're dancing all night! Yee-Haw!*

When it became apparent that the coach was perfectly capable and willing to continue his part in this preposterous dance, I called the moms into a quick huddle, but it was Cybil that did all the talking.

"Ok, this clearly isn't working. We need to fan out and confuse him. Drive him to the right and then cut him off short. Push him in my direction. I'll get him toward the tree line where the field drops off. Game ends here, ladies. That bastard's mine. He's going down!"

The 4th quarter of the game against the Mustangs was intense! Our players were hitting hard, both teams were playing a little bit dirty, and we were leading by 2 points with less than 4 minutes left in the game. Unfortunately for the Ravens coach, he couldn't quite see the game from his newly acquired vantage point. He had tried to pull an impressive donut maneuver in his wheelchair in attempt to shake Cybil at the tree line, but by the time he realized the ground dropped at that particular spot on the field, there was little he could do but brace himself for the fall. I guess that's what they mean by using your "home field advantage".

No one disrespects us in our house! Cybil shrieked inside my head with a triumphant war cry as she watched the Ravens coach lose his heroic fight.

His wheelchair made a very satisfying *ssschlepppp* sound when its front wheels finally hit a juicy spot of mud. The front wheels sunk just far enough for the back wheels to lift a few inches off the ground and continue to spin in dead air. He finally lost his very noble fight against gravity and the mushy terrain as the wheelchair tipped over and started to sink in the gooey mud.

The *good news* was that the Ravens coach was not at all injured and was only partially covered in mud. The *bad news* was he wasn't going to be able to extricate the chair or get back in it without some assistance. The *worst news* of all, however, and very unfortunate for him, was that Cybil apparently suffers from a very short attention span and didn't remember to mention to anyone that he needed help.

Cybil and I returned to our game against the Mustangs and noticed my son sitting on the bench with the rest of the players receiving their instructions for the final play of the game. Ignoring the warning look my husband was giving me, I watched as Cybil approached the players on the bench. Cybil had worked too hard to get this far in the football season and would be damned if she was going to just sit by and watch the team lose the game now. Cybil grabbed my son hard by the face mask and pulled him right into her face so she could impart a few motivating words of encouragement:

"This is it! This is your game! You get in that kid's face and you tell that boy that you are here today to make him cry! You put that frickin' kid in the ground, you understand?"

I guess on some level my thoughts and behaviors may appear to have been a little over the top, but like I said, I think it only sounds bad because I'm verbalizing it out loud. It all sounds perfectly normal in my head.

My son's football team ended up going to the playoffs with an impressive record of 11 wins 1 loss 0 ties. We were officially a better football team than the Washington Redskins or the Dallas Cowboys!

Will my son play football again next year? I'm not sure. My son hasn't quite committed to it yet and for whatever reason, my husband has gotten pretty quiet about the whole sports topic around me.

5 PUSSY HARD TO SWALLOW & WHY I CAN NO LONGER EAT OREO COOKIES

We've all heard someone claim that they are a "people person". They spew on and on about how much they love being around people and how much they love helping people. These people lovers will tell you they don't need money or fame. All they need to be happy is the satisfaction of knowing they are helping others and making a difference in people's lives. They will tell you that they get great satisfaction from spending their days serving other people. You know what else? These people are lying to you. Flat out lying. No one in the real world who has ever worked longer than 15 minutes in a row with people likes people. Any time a person tells you they are a people person, it means only 1 of

2 things: 1. they've never actually spent much time around other people or 2. they're lying.

How do I know this? I know this because I am one of these people persons. I am a true people person to the core. I am a Pisces. My destiny as a natural born people person was cast in the stars the night my mother brought me into this world, so I've never stood a chance. Anyone who is a Pisces or knows a Pisces knows that the sensitive and gullible people born under this sign are cursed with a gift that attracts all people to them. And I am no ordinary Pisces. I am the very special breed of Pisces that sends out pulsing signals that scream *come talk to me about all your personal problems! I want to help you! I need to help you!* Anxious, depressed, psychotic, lunatic, bipolar, manic - you name it, I attract it. Perhaps you've heard of me? In some circles I am known as the Pied Piper of Mental Illness.

Crazy people will literally come crawling out of the bowels of the Earth to make their way to me. They are hopelessly attracted to me the same way flies are hopelessly attracted to a pile of shit. I am a living, breathing, steaming, pile of shit - the kind that's topped off by that cute little swirl on top.

My high school guidance counselor was probably one of the first adults in my life to recognize this people magnet in me and it was he who helped influence and shape the path my future would take.

"You have an amazing gift... you seem to really care about other people... you're so genuine about your concern and wanting to help people... you just absolutely *have* to do something that involves working intimately with people."

Thanks in part to his guidance and my inability to master advanced high school math or science, I convinced myself that I would be happy only if I ended up in a job where I could work intimately with people and make them better. So fast forward 20 years later into my people person career and ask me if I still like working with people. You might be shocked to learn that I do. After all these years, I still like people. You know what kind of people are my favorites? The dead ones.

And for the record, my high school guidance counselor will be the first victim on my to-do list the day I decide to kick-off my new career as a serial killer, which I guess technically still falls under a people person type of career.

True to my Piscean nature and the guidance of my high school counselor, I dove into the whole people person career dream head first. I spent my senior year in high school researching universities and zeroing in on degrees that didn't involve advanced math or science. After months of research, I decided on Arizona State University (ASU) in the beautiful, sunny Tempe, Arizona. Back in the day when I was a student, ASU wasn't exactly famous for churning out rocket scientists, and therefore was the perfect choice for me. ASU was, however, known for its fraternity parties, sorority parties, dorm parties, concerts, clubs and bars, which were all conveniently located within drunken stumbling distance from campus. So pretty typical for many of its student population, my first - which would also turn out to be my last - year at ASU was spent in one big, intoxicated blur.

I still don't have very clear memories of things that transpired my freshman year, but I do vividly recall the *come-to-Jesus* session with my parental units after they received my 2nd report card reflecting a very impressive grade point average of 1.8 on a 4.0 scale. And by *impressive*

I mean it's impressive that I managed to earn a grade point average at all considering what I'd been up to, which even I'm not stupid enough to put in writing.

"What the hell have you been doing? Christ almighty, what's this shit I've been paying for?" my not-so-Catholic father screamed at me.

For those of you Next Gen and Millennium kids who've never heard a parent scream or say anything remotely critical to you for fear of traumatizing your oh-so-sensitive natures, let me translate my dad's reaction into the language you may be more familiar with:

"We're not disappointed in *you*, we're disappointed in the *situation*. We should consider this a great learning opportunity... we love you and believe in you because you're a winner! Mom and I have discussed it at length and we agree that this would be the right time for you to explore some alternative avenues for financing your college education..."

I took my parent's advice and I started doing some serious thinking and exploring of other opportunities for financing my college. I started as most normal female teenagers would - at the shopping mall. It was probably no coincidence that the shopping mall closest to ASU campus conveniently housed military recruiting posts for all branches of the armed forces. I imagine it was like fishing in a bucket for these military recruiters. Hell, they didn't even have to try. All they had to do was sit back and wait for report card time and all the college drop-outs from ASU to show up begging at their door.

I decided I was going to be smarter than the average college drop-out about my approach in joining the military and I decided the best approach would be for me to visit each branch and see what they were about. I was going to use the "Goldie Locks and the Three Bears" strategy and visit each one and sample everything they had to offer.

The first door I came across was the Navy recruiting post. That one wasn't hard for me to immediately rule out. Believe it or not, the Navy had a swimming requirement. I grew up in a desert. I can't swim. I don't like swimming and I don't think it's natural to be in or on top of water. I don't do swimming pools, ponds, hot tubs, streams, oceans, lakes, or any body of water, especially if I can't see what lurks beneath it. I told the Navy recruiter that I could possibly doggie paddle for a few seconds, but the moment I felt my face start to go under water or my hair got wet and started to frizz up, I would most likely surrender the ship and shipmates to the enemies - no torture required. The recruiter and I both agreed that the Navy probably wouldn't be a good fit for me. He laughed a little as he recommended the Army recruiting center should be my next stop.

The Army. Wow. God bless the men and women in the Army. I couldn't do it. And by "it" I mean I couldn't do 5 pushups, so never mind getting up at the crack of dawn and "humping" - whatever that meant. The recruiter must have used the word "humping" 20 times in our conversation: *we pack our gear and hump here and hump there...* I'm pretty sure I wasn't humping material. My next stop: the Marines.

I flounced in the Marine recruiting center wearing my 1980's orange day-glow shorts, "Frankie Says Relax!" t-shirt, and flip-flops. In one hand I was holding the strawberry smoothie I bought at the food court in the mall and in the other hand I was holding my berrylicous flavored lip-gloss. I'm lucky I made it out of there alive.

That Marine looked like he could have killed me with the plastic straw sticking out of my smoothie. I take that back. That Marine looked like he wanted to kill me, was looking forward to killing me, with the plastic straw sticking out of my strawberry smoothie. Next stop: Air Force.

The Air Force was exactly what I was looking for and was definitely more my speed - no swimming, no humping, no haircut required. I could still wear my lip-gloss, and they would help me pay for college. And if that wasn't enough, the Air Force also promised me the perfect people person type of career. They were looking for sensitive and caring people lovers like me to serve as Medics in their hospitals! I signed the Air Force contract on the spot, and 3 weeks later I was on a bus headed to San Antonio, Texas, excited about kicking off my new people person career as a Medic.

This point in my very inexperienced life also coincided with the airing of the popular television show "E.R." and I, like millions of other viewers, was hooked. I admit the appeal of this show may have had a little something to do with George Clooney, the irrepressible, gorgeous, and brilliant Doctor Ross. I was mesmerized by his unwavering compassion and his ability to save people's lives. No matter how far-fetched or unknown a patient's medical affliction, they would miraculously pull through just in time for the last commercial thanks to the oh-so-sexy Dr. Ross and his supporting cast. I stood no fighting chance. The devoted and heroic Dr. Ross, the satisfaction of knowing I would be just like him, helping the grateful people who would love and appreciate me - the lure of living this fantasy was like crack cocaine to an addict.

If I had spent a little more time reading the entire Pisces horoscope, maybe I would have come across one particular little nugget of information about myself that may have saved me much frustration later on in life. Apparently I and my Piscean brethren suffer from a very serious "Achilles heel", which is our tendency to dally in a dream world. And dream I did. The day I got my Medic orders in my hot little hands, I got my head stuck up in the clouds, fantasizing about how I would be working in a hospital alongside a real life Dr. Ross. I was going to be the modern-day Florence Nightengale! I would be a servant to the people and the people would love me!

I was shocked to discover that the real world emergency room was nothing like my Dr. Ross fantasy or the "E.R." television show. In fact, little by little, I came to discover that pretty much everything I fell in love with on the "E.R." episodes turned out to be Hollywood bullshit. For starters, none of the doctors in the military emergency room even looked remotely like Dr. Ross or had easy-to-pronounce American names like "Ross".

"E.R." also brainwashed me week after week into believing that a hospital emergency room would be one big, exciting, non-stop, life-or-death situation. I was very dismayed to discover that in the real world, emergency rooms are swamped by an endless flow of not-exciting-enough-for-television-crap. We'd spend a lot of time treating patients with unexplainable rashes, stomach aches, joint pain, fevers, cold symptoms, and yeast infections. Sprinkle a little mental illness into that mix, and I wasn't exactly off to a very promising start on my whole people person fantasy career.

You know what I've never seen on an episode of "E.R."? I've never seen the charming Dr. Ross and his assistant dressed in surgical gowns prepared to go fishing for treasure up another person's ass. But in the real world emergency room, we did that at least 2 times per shift, and that was on a slow weekend.

"Come on, you know the routine: slap a snorkel on me, tie a rope securely around my waist – I'm going in! If you feel me tug 2 times on the rope, for Chrissakes, pull me out! Don't let me die in there!"

That would be the half-joking instructions I'd get from a real world physician as we gowned up for our next cavernous dive. Just another poor, disillusioned people person struggling with the realization that he spent years attending Ivy League universities in his noble quest to save lives, but now spends half his time extracting small household appliances from people's asses. You would think a diploma from a less prestigious institution or a technical training college would have sufficed.

For me, my assignment in the emergency room was my introduction to the real world of working with real people. My experience awarded me an education like no fancy college degree ever could. It was quick, hard, and dirty. No one bought me flowers or took me out to a fancy dinner. I got no kiss on the lips or a promise they'd call me the next day. I wasn't even offered any lubricant. I was simply bent over and they drove it straight in. And what does any of this have to do with pussy and Oreo cookies? Won't you please join me on a quick flashback and I'll see if I can answer these questions for you...

I was working the emergency room night shift when our pussy problem patient arrived via ambulance. This was summer time in Texas. It was hot. Texas hot. One-hundred-and-ten degrees, ninety-nine percent humidity hot. This patient arrived in the form of a huge mass of pasty white flesh covered in sweat. I don't mean her body was glistening in sexy little beads of perspiration. I mean this woman was sweating like the pig who knows she's supper, as the saying goes in the South. Her hair was long and stringy and it lay plastered to her head and shoulders, and from where I stood many feet away, I could smell an odor coming off her like milk gone sour.

Some of you reading this may be giggling a little, feeling a little guilty for doing so, as you nervously anticipate a dirty sexual story starring this obese woman and an Oreo cookie. For the rest of you reading this - you *normal* people - I have already undoubtedly offended you by crossing that line and insulting an obese person. Before you judge me too harshly, you should know that in the 8 years I spent working in a hospital trying to live my dream of helping the good people of this Earth, I have been spit on, urinated on, slapped, and pinched. I've had human feces deliberately smeared on me, and I've had my hair pulled out by the fistful. I've been bitten, kicked, and called every offensive name you can think of in just about every language or dialect known to mankind. I've been groped, kissed, and felt-up more times than I can remember or therapy will ever let me forget. So if you're going to feel sorry for anyone in this story, it should be me. I'm the victim here. It was my dream - not *Ms. I've got a pussy problem's* - that died that night in the emergency room.

I don't know why after all the years I spent in the hospital, after all the things I'd seen and smelled - after all the abuse at the hands of patients I was trying to help - I don't know why this particular night or this particular woman was the proverbial straw that broke my back. Maybe it wasn't her at all. Maybe it was just bad timing. Or maybe it was the culmination of everything over the last 8 years and by the time she rolled in,

I had just reached my breaking point. Or maybe the careless and senseless despoiling of an iconic American symbol like the Oreo cookie was just too much for me to bear and I just snapped.

Regardless of whatever *it* was, there I stood in the emergency room as the ambulance EMTs rolled this woman in, happy that they would be dumping her off on me.

> "Oh, please God, no....Oh, please God, I promise to get back to Church. Please God don't let there be an animal stuck up inside her", I silently prayed as the doctor and I stood in mute horror waiting to receive her.

The ambulance crew had covered her with the stale-smelling flowered sheets from her king sized bed at home because her body was too large to cover with even 3 hospital gowns. We weren't able to get an official weight on her as we didn't have a scale that could handle that kind of body mass, but she must have weighed over seven-hundred pounds. It took 6 grown men, 3 hospital sheets, 2 gurney restraints, and 1 manual crane-lift to transfer her onto 2 extra-wide exam tables we had shoved together. And even with our makeshift accommodations, 1 entire side of her body still hung off the exam table, draping it in flabby folds like a table cloth made of human flesh. The ambulance crew laughed and made their rapid retreat as they wished me luck on helping this woman out with her "pussy problem".

"OhJesusChristpeddlingonabicycle! Please kill me now!" the doctor blasphemed as we read the documented reasons our patient gave for calling 911 and having an ambulance transport her to our E.R.:

1) I can't go to the bathroom - extremely constipated. 2) My throat - pussy hard to swallow.

Well, God bless Texas and Texas public education. I think it may have been that very moment when I first heard the distant sound of my little dream bubble popping inside my head. This woman was trying to tell us that her throat was full of pus. She was trying to impart that her throat was *pus-see,* but her intended meaning was clearly lost in translation.

Pussy is perhaps the one word in the English language that is used in the wrong context more often than any other word. We saw the word *pussy* misused more often than the word *diarrhea* was misspelled. Just to set the record straight and possibly save you from an embarrassing session with a doctor some day in your future - there is no such word as *pussy* in the sense of something containing pus. Something infected and containing pus is referred to as *containing pus* or being *purulent*. You should only use the word *pussy* if you are looking for a referral to a good Gynecologist.

So, to summarize, a human throat can be purulent or the throat may contain pus, but unless something really kinky is going on, chances are female genitalia will not be impacting your ability to swallow. Now, if by some wild chance the aforementioned is in fact what's going on and you find yourself in a precarious *pussy hard to swallow* situation requiring emergency medical treatment, please do us all a favor and just stay home. Save yourself and your poor Catholic martyr-of-a-mother the humiliation and embarrassment. Just lay down wherever you happen to be afflicted by your pussy situation, make yourself comfortable, and die.

The good news for us was that pussy was not literally what this gigantic patient of ours had going on in her throat. And to that all I can say is *thank you God for small favors*! The bad news for us was that since she complained of being severely constipated, we were required to perform a rectal exam, which meant even though we were spared getting up close and personal with her pussy, we were not going to be spared her cavernous ass.

"Hey, Doc, you ready to throw on your snorkeling gear and do some deep-cave diving?"

"Oh bite me! I knew I should have been a fucking Dermatologist. Let's go get this shit over with."

The doctor had a miserable look on his face as we gowned up and mentally tried to prepare ourselves to conduct a professional and compassionate exam. My immediate task in assisting the doctor in this kind of exam was to position our enormous patient onto her side so the doctor could insert his finger up her rectum. She kept crying and complaining that she was in too much discomfort to move herself and I didn't know how I was going to possibly move or roll her into position. In the end we agreed we would try it together, so I started by tugging and pulling on the bed sheet in an attempt to first dislodge it from where it had been half swallowed by her enormous butt cheeks.

While I was pulling and tugging, her job was to try to heave her body onto her side. I dug my heels into the floor for traction and I strained to pull the sheet out from under her. With every pull on the sheet I tried to remind myself that this was a human being needing my help and I should be sensitive and compassionate. But with every pull, her body convulsed and her fat rolls rippled and rolled. With every movement she forced herself to make, she groaned and farted a rotting smell of decay right in my face. Under my breath I vowed to myself and the doctor, "I'm so quitting this job... I can't do this another day... I'm so quitting this job... I'm so quitting this job..."

Finally, with one angry and explosive heave, I succeeded in freeing the bed sheet out from under her butt and wrestled her onto her side. I was terrified that she would slip off the exam table and hit the floor, but there was no way in hell I was going to throw my body in front of her to break the fall. I have to admit that for a split-second I did fantasize about giving her a little nudge off the exam table - if we were lucky she'd land on her head and we could skip the rectal exam altogether and transfer her directly to the Neurology ward.

Fortunately for our patient, my people person gene kicked in and I didn't push her off the table. And as she didn't end up falling off the exam table on her own, we were stuck with her in the E.R. Once she was positioned on her side, I held my hands against her sweaty, slippery back to prevent her from rolling backwards off the table. Her gigantic breasts, which were literally larger than the size of most human heads, heaved and shook with every movement. When she finally collapsed into a resting position, out from under one mammoth breast fell an Oreo cookie. I repeat: out from under her mammoth breast fell an Oreo cookie.

I'd seen a lot of things in my years working in a hospital, but I'd never seen a woman dispense cookies from her breast. This was definitely a medical first. The Oreo rolling out from under her breast reminded me of the kid's song "I Lost My Poor Meatball" and I started humming it to myself: *It rolled off the table and onto the floor and then my poor meatball rolled right out...* At least, I hoped I was humming it to myself.

Now, I know what some of you are thinking and I'm way ahead of you: How much would Nabisco Corporation pay for this great, original idea for their next cookie commercial?

"Hey kids! You and your moms know that Oreos go great with a cold glass of milk, but did you know that Oreos can be conveniently tucked away under your flabby folds of fat to enjoy later? Just cram them up in your fat ass and jiggle 'em out..."

As I stood too stunned to initially react, the doctor calmly reached down to the floor where the Oreo had stopped rolling, picked it up, and handed it to me. Caught off guard, I reached out with my un-gloved hand to accept it. I could feel the cookie was turning a little soft and it felt a little slimy from where it had been pooling in the sweat under her breast. I was also horrified to see that there was a light green, hairy fluff of some lint-like substance clinging to the creamy filling, which happens to be my absolute favorite part of the entire Oreo experience.

I can't even walk around with a tiny pebble in my shoe, so how this woman could live with a cookie lodged under her boob was beyond me. What had this crazy walrus of a woman done?

She had taken this amazing American icon with its crunchy chocolaty exterior filled with its oh-so-creamy-goodness and had completely desecrated it. The thought of that poor little defenseless Oreo just crammed up in there, slowly suffocating and putrefying under the folds of her fat, turning milky grey and slimy...

"Hey, you gonna eat that cookie or can I have it?" the doctor joked, startling me back to the present.

I gagged and fought to hold back the vomit as I pictured myself placing that slimy, fuzzy Oreo in my mouth.

"I'll give you $20 if you take a lick right out of the center of that Oreo", the doctor continued to tease me as he removed his finger from the patient's ass.

I didn't know if I wanted to vomit first or go grab a broomstick from the janitor's closet and smack this fat woman.

I just felt like I needed to give her a few solid whacks with a stick to see if I could make more cookies fall out of her like some mammoth piñata.

And that's a sign, folks. When you start fantasizing about turning your patients into living human piñatas, the Florence Nightengale people person loving dream is officially over.

Time to move on.

6 EXACTLY LIKE PRISON MINUS THE FREE SEX

Once upon a time, I used to think the scariest day in my adult life would be the day my child sought me out for fashion assistance on Dress like a Geek day at school.

"Hey mom, it's Geek Day, can I borrow some of your clothes? No, not your old stuff! The stuff you wear every day is just perfect!"

I now realize that scarier than Geek Day is Career Day where parents are invited to visit their child's classroom to talk about their jobs and what they do all day at work. I don't know which I find more upsetting – the fact that Career Day exists at all or the fact that after my last

Career Day speaking engagement, my child has never invited me to return to speak about my job. Honestly, it's hard enough trying to explain and justify the existence of federal government bureaucracy to another adult, tax-paying citizen, but it's almost impossible to explain it to a 5th grade class of 12 year olds without sounding like your job is lame and unnecessary.

> "Well, let's see, I arrive to my office and then I say good morning to some of my colleagues and then I go grab a cup of coffee. Then I check my emails and I answer some phone calls and then I get ready to attend 5 or sometimes 6 meetings. And then I … um … did I already say I go grab a cup of coffee?"

Oh yaaaaawn. Is anyone out there still awake?

Back in the day when I was a Medic in the Air Force, I used to have a huge collection of very exciting stories to share with a classroom full of kids. I had countless funny, gory, disgustingly horrific stories, practically guaranteed to make 2 children per Career Day speech throw up their lunch.

One of my assignments as a Medic was on the hospital's in-patient urology ward. For those of you who may not be familiar, urology is the practice that specializes in dealing with the urinary system (your pee-pee tubes), urinary organs (your pee-pee), and all their associated disorders and malfunctions (gross and yuck). Let me paint you a picture: At this point in my career, I was a 23 year old girl trapped on a forty-eight bed hospital ward that was ninety-nine percent occupied by men and their penis problems. The average age of my male patients on this ward was between the ages of sixty-five and dead.

I was completely and hopelessly surrounded by old-man dick. All day, every day, for 12-hours per shift. Old, floppy, wrinkled dick. Uncircumcised, circumcised, flaccid, and sagging…then there were rigid and drippy and swollen and inverted… I was literally living the Snow-White-and-the-Penis-Dwarves-You-Never-Wanted-to-Meet fairy tale.

Not to brag, but when it comes to the penis, you name it, I've seen it. Chances are at some point along the way, I've even been required to hold it in my hands. Pay close attention, kids, and believe me when I tell you that the military medical recruiters conveniently forget to share that one particular glamorous detail with you when they set up their *Discover Your Life-Long Career as a Medic!* recruiting booth in the high school cafeteria. Please allow me to also put to rest perhaps one of the most pervasive and inaccurate myths out there: after many years of working intimately with naked men I can tell you with a great amount of confidence that a large pair of shoes on a man means he's packing a very large pair of socks, and that's about it. Sorry to kill the fantasy.

After all these years what I still don't understand is why on earth the U.S. Government would waste billions of research dollars on penis pumps and sexual enhancement drugs. The only explanation that makes any sense to me is that these items are the ridiculous inventions of some deranged *male* scientist. Have you ever seen a wrinkled eighty year-old man with his shriveled, liver-spotted ass sticking out the back of a hospital gown? Envision that old man and his 2 inch penis - that's fully erect, folks - shuffling down the hospital hallway in his slippers, dragging on the floor behind him approximately 10 pounds of sweaty, wrinkled, grey-haired, bean bag. There's no way in hell any *female* scientist in this galaxy witnessed that sickening spectacle and thought, *Eureka! If only he had an implant that allowed him to pump up his penis at-will and keep it erect for 6 to 8 hours!*

To say I was traumatized by the years I spent working with naked old men would be an understatement. No amount of showering, pills, or booze will ever erase the visions of saggy penis and wrinkled bean bag that has been burned into my brain.

After leaving the military, I simply wanted to land a job where I no longer had to look at naked people. I wanted a predictable, steady, normal job. And what could possibly be more *normal* than a job with the federal government? (inscrt drum sound that follows a corny joke here)

Before I landed my government job, I was thinking the exact same thing you're probably thinking right now about the government and federal employees. In fact, many of my friends and family tried to talk me out of pursuing a job with the government, warning me that I didn't have the personality or patience for it. However, the lure of working in a nice, climate controlled office environment with people who would never be naked in front of me was just too tempting and I couldn't resist.

In the years I've been a federal employee, I've learned that federal government work really isn't that different from other work. Sure, the work may take a little longer to get done, and maybe sometimes it costs a few dollars more than we'd typically expect, but work is work. I understand why the public loves to poke fun at the federal employee stereotype, but let's be honest, even the best companies out there have dead-weight douche bags on their payroll. I bet you can think of at least 3 people you work with right now who fit that job description. The dead-weight douche bag isn't indigenous to government and the federal government certainly didn't invent it. Actually, I think it was invented by Al Gore, the same year he invented the Internet.

I consider myself to be one of the lucky federal employees. I don't work for some mess like FEMA or some place with make-believe jobs like Minerals Management. *Managing minerals?* Really? The last time I checked, which was admittedly 5th grade science class, minerals could manage to grow themselves without any oversight from the federal government whatsoever.

I am employed by one of the best federal agencies out there. Every day I get to work with the smartest men and women you'll ever meet. Not to give away too much, but in my agency you may overhear words like *nuclear propulsion, Mars, or black hole.* These people I work with are brilliant. I am not. I'd be the federal employee sitting in that meeting giggling, *tee-hee-hee, he said hole!*

Brilliant or not, the people I work with are still federal employees at heart, and as such, there is nothing we love more than a meeting. We'll even schedule a meeting to talk about what we're going to talk about at a future meeting. And I don't just attend meetings. I also attend tag-ups, teleconferences, brain-storming sessions, video conferences, discussions, project kick-offs, focus group sessions... I think you get the picture.

It's typically somewhere around my 4th meeting of the day when my non-brilliant brain starts to give out on me and I slowly start to shut down. This is usually the point in a meeting where I start doodling, compiling grocery lists, or fantasizing about the day Brad dumps Angelina and she comes running to me, finally realizing that I am the woman she's been waiting for her entire life. Angelina Jolie. Hot damn! Don't tell my husband I said so, but I'd switch teams in half a heart beat for that woman.

Sometimes I'll sit in a meeting and I'll reminisce about something bizarre like the weirdest job perk in all of federal government: the Mammo Van. Yes, you read that correctly. The Mammo Van is literally a van that parks right outside my office in the middle of downtown Washington, D.C., and performs free mobile breast exams and *mammographs? mammographies? mammograms?* I really don't know what the exam is called - anatomical appendages above the waist weren't exactly my medical specialty.

The Mammo Van is a large, inconspicuous white van which thankfully does not have the words "Mammo Van!" splashed all over it for all of D.C. to read. However, because it does look pretty similar to a lot of other vans driving around downtown, I've learned I have to be careful and make sure that I walk into the correct van before I start undressing, otherwise it makes for a pretty awkward introduction. Thank goodness President Obama doesn't ride around D.C. in a white van motorcade, otherwise I imagine it's just a matter of time before I jump into his van by mistake and start to strip naked. That would not be good. After all, this isn't Bill Clinton's presidency we're talking about here.

Obama's secret service would taser my ass to the ground before they let me unleash my boobs on him.

While I'm standing naked in the Mammo Van with my boobs smashed in a vise grip there are cars, pedestrians, and bicyclists rushing all around. The sounds of screeching tires and cab drivers blaring their horns and cussing at each other makes me feel a little nervous about my predicament as I imagine things that could go wrong. *What if someone crashes into us and sends us spinning out into traffic? What if the driver forgot to engage the parking brake and we go rolling down the street? What if the technicians didn't feed the parking meter and we were towed away with me half-naked and trapped inside?*

So these are some of the non-brilliant thoughts that go through my head as I sit in some of my daily meetings. I honestly don't remember which meeting I was sitting in one day when my mind really started to wander, but I am positive that it was not a meeting with my supervisor - hey, I may not be normal, but I'm not stupid. I started thinking about some of the stuff that I've experienced in the years I've been a federal employee and the more I thought about it, the more convinced I became that I was on to something. I couldn't believe it took me this many years to figure it out, but as soon as the thought took shape in my head, I knew it was true: federal employees are prisoners! Being a federal employee is exactly like being a federal prisoner, except we don't get any of that free prison sex.

The federal government office environment, just like a federal prison, is full of *lifers* – people who have spent their entire lives and have exhausted their youth incarcerated within the confines of their respective federally funded institutions. Lifers spend their current existence counting down the days. They track the time they've already served toward their sentence and they count down the days to their release from captivity. Oh sure, in the federal government they may call it *retirement eligibility*, but I refuse to be fooled by the semantics. Retirement eligibility, parole, release, escape – no matter what you call it, it's still the legally binding day some designated federal officer has determined to be my authorized release from captivity. And believe me, they've got it calculated down to the exact hour on the exact day, on the exact month, and on the exact year I am to be released, and they will not authorize my release one minute sooner.

Confinement to a small, unattractive space is another glaring similarity shared between the federal government employee and the federal prisoner. We both spend the majority of our days confined in small spaces containing no windows or doors leading to the outside world. I consulted the dictionary and discovered that the words Webster uses to describe a prison cell can easily be used to describe my office cubicle. According to the dictionary, a prison cell is a generally small enclosure with 3 hard walls and an open side secured with some kind of door to prevent escape. Well, my office cubicle is also a small enclosure with 3 hard walls. The only difference between the prison cell and my cubicle is that my open side contains a sliding plastic door. I'd like to think that the door's purpose on my cubicle isn't to prevent my escape, but how can I possibly be sure? I mean, I didn't even know I was a prisoner until just recently.

Prison cells and office cubicles are also similar in their construction in the sense that they both contain furnishings that have been anchored to a wall or floor. Whether it's the sink and toilet in a prison cell, or the desk and cabinets in a cubicle, federal employees and prisoners alike are prohibited from rearranging the furnishings. We are both purposefully prevented from moving the fixtures or furnishings within our confined spaces to our personal preference.

Both prisoners and federal employees also enjoy similar amenities, a number of them at no cost to them thanks to the taxpayers' contributions. We both get free unlimited access to the internet, access to an onsite health clinic, unlimited library resources, and some also enjoy free gym memberships.

Similarities aside, there is one very inequitable perk that federal prisoners can look forward to that does not apply to federal government employees like me. I'm not referring to the free prison sex here either. I'm talking about the opportunity to get credit for good behavior during time served and get an early release.

We've all heard how the system works - a violent felon is sentenced to serve thirty years in a federal prison, but at the 5 year mark into the prisoner's sentence, it's discovered that they've been on good behavior and they're set free early. A prisoner can serve a fraction of their sentence and simply because they managed not to shank someone during that time, they're set free. That is completely unfair. I've managed to make it through 12 years in a row of being a federal employee and I haven't shanked anyone in my office yet, but you don't see anyone letting me out of my sentence early.

According to my latest calculations, I have another 18 years to go before they allow me to go free. But because I am a federal government employee and not a federal prisoner, I stand no chance for early release. So here I sit, and I will continue to sit, quietly serving my time, for the next 7,456 days, 13 hours, 24 minutes, and 35 seconds.

But then again, who's counting?

7 GETTING MY KICKS ON ROUTE 666

As my last defiant gesture - my middle finger thrust to the world - I fully intend to lay my dying ass down smack in the middle of the freeway in full-blown Washington, D.C. rush-hour traffic. Dead or not, I am absolutely looking forward to this one opportunity for me to finally screw up someone else's commute for a change.

02:30 a.m. and I'm tossing and turning.

02:45 a.m. and I've rolled away from my husband in search of cooler sheets on the far side of the bed.

I throw off the covers, reposition myself and attempt to immediately fall back asleep.

03:00 a.m. according to the alarm clock that is mocking me with the reality that I will be dead on my feet tomorrow unless I fall asleep *right now!*

03:15 a.m.

03:30 a.m.

03:45 a.m.

At 03:50 a.m. I sigh loudly and roll over for the final time, reaching out to disarm the alarm clock and prevent it from ringing at its programmed 04:00 a.m. wake-up time.

04:00-fucking-a.m. I can't believe it's even legal to refer to that particular time of day as "a.m."

I sit on the edge of the bed half awake, muttering a few colorful choice words under my breath, slightly annoyed that my husband doesn't have to be up at this hour. I look at my husband's face, peaceful in sleep, and I give the covers a sharp tug, secretly hoping to disturb his slumber. Within seconds I hear the voices inside my head start their semi-coherent whining. *This sucks! What the hell am I doing? I can't believe I have to get up. This is ridiculous! Why do I have to get up at this rotten time of day?* Sarah Palin, that's why. Oh yeah, I said it. It's Sarah Palin's fault. It's her and the rest of this new super-breed of women out there just like her.

You know the type of woman I'm talking about. They can't just be pretty, they're *beautiful*. They can't just have a job, they have high-power, high-pressure, ball-busting *careers*. On the home front, these women are super-mommies not to just 1 or 2, but to *litters*, of children. They are the perfect party hostesses, Chairmen of the school PTAs, they organize fund raising activities, and they run for every cure. And in their spare time they're ready to run the damn Country. Screw them! I don't need this kind of pressure!

With my plain, regular job and my one child to assist with homework in the evenings, I struggle to keep it all together. When my son threw in one after-school activity, on most nights I couldn't even pull off cooking dinner.

I sigh loudly again, stretch, and prepare to get myself up and around for the day as the voices in my head continue to scold me. *You should have spent less money on college and more on plastic surgery. Why did you marry for love? Had you landed yourself some rich old geezer you wouldn't have to be getting up at this God forsaken time of day.* But since I didn't land myself a rich old geezer, I resign myself to waking up at the insane hour of 04:00 a.m. to head into work with the millions of other ill-fated commuters in the Washington, D.C. metro area.

Just about every major U.S. city or state is known for something. Minnesota, for example, has the world's largest ball of twine and New York City has the Statue of Liberty. Texas has the Alamo, and Arizona has the Grand Canyon. When most people think of Washington, D.C. they immediately think of the White House, Congress, the monuments, or the museums. But to us locals, the commute in D.C. is first and foremost on our minds. The commute in D.C. entangles the entire Northern Virginia, Maryland, and D.C. metropolitan area and it is a vile, pervasive presence in our lives that causes immeasurable stress, anxiety, and frustration.

The sheer volume of traffic alone going in and out of D.C. can be intimidating to even a very experienced driver, but when you throw in the unpredictability of the thousands of Pakistani cab drivers and Saudi women learning to drive cars at the same time they're learning to decipher English traffic signs, it's downright terrifying. Rush hour, car accidents, speed traps, late nights, early mornings, light drizzle, pouring rain, fog, sun glare, global warming, free range chickens, the wind is blowing, Lindsay Lohan is back in rehab, Paris Hilton has a new best friend - absolutely *any excuse at all* will do to completely screw up the commute in D.C

D.C. locals spend hours each day commuting to and from work, averaging between 1 and 2 hours each way. Let me do the math for you: 2 to 4 hours every day comes to 10 to 20 hours per week, which equals eighty-hours per month. That's nine-hundred-and-sixty-hours per year spent commuting. Commuters in D.C spend *nine-hundred-and-sixty-hours* per year doing nothing else but commuting to and from work. And that's if and only if traffic is actually moving.

How can D.C. commuters tolerate this miserable existence? What could possibly motivate us to put up with such a wretched commute? Given how early we have to go to bed and wake up, commuting is the only life experience some of us have outside of work. Commuting is practically my hobby. And though we all claim to hate the D.C. commute, secretly we derive a sick sense of pleasure from it. We're absolute masochists. Some of us are such extreme commuting masochists that we'll even dedicate a whole chapter in a book to the subject.

Victims and veterans of the D.C. commute share their traumatic commuting experiences using the same hushed, reverent tone of voice one reserves for discussing horrific subjects like Catholic priests molesting little boys or Joan River's latest nose job (*author's note: my first draft reflected Michael Jackson's latest nose job, but because I'm superstitious about talking shit about the dead, I had to do a quick re-write. I just hope people reading this know who Joan Rivers is.)

We D.C. commuters live to tell our commuting horror stories and we will share them with absolutely anyone who will listen. We are such commuting connoisseurs that we actually compete among each other to see who suffers from the worst commute. The morning ritual in every D.C. office building is pretty much the same no matter where I've worked. As soon as I arrive in the office I hit the door in a panicked rush to find a bathroom since I've been trapped in a vehicle the last 2 hours, then I go grab a cup of coffee with some coworkers and we spend the next hour reliving our commuting horror stories. The winner of this sick commuting contest gets full bragging rights and gets to wear a *commuting masochist* medal of honor until the next day when someone else's commute inevitably turns out to be worse.

Perhaps the scariest element of the D.C commute is being stuck in rush-hour traffic surrounded by Sarah Palin wannabes commandeering 2-ton SUVs. These women are powerhouse multi-taskers who spend every morning and evening rushing in and out of D.C. traffic. They've got their perfect, gifted children strapped in safety harnesses in their back seats with age-appropriate entertainment playing on their DVDs as they talk on their cell phones, drink their coffee, and cut-off other drivers.

This dirver is aggressive and will do whatever it takes to maneuver through D.C. traffic in order to stay on task with her busy work and household schedules. Never mind terrorists, the FBI, or undercover CIA operatives - there is no one in D.C. that you should fear more. She rushes to drop off children at school, rushes to get to work, rushes to leave work, and rushes to pick up kids. In the midst of it all, she drops off dry-cleaning, picks up groceries, and attends a kindergarten graduation ceremony. She speeds in and out of D.C. in order to get all her errands done, make it home in time to cook dinner, get homework completed, lunches packed, and get the kids to bed so she can wake up the next morning at 04:00 a.m. to start the cycle all over again.

This Sarah Palin wannabe in her gas guzzling SUV is an intimidating, commendable force to be reckoned with. The day some poor wretch of a human being decides to jump off a D.C. bridge and end their life, I know 3 things for certain:

1. they better not do it during morning or evening rush hour

2. they better do it expediently

3. they better not change their mind

The moment that person climbs that bridge threatening to end their life and the police start slowing down D.C. traffic, if that person knows what's good for them, they better jump. Otherwise, some D.C. commuting super-mommy is going to get out of her luxury SUV and make that person wish they'd jumped. She's going to scale that bridge in precisely 5 seconds flat wearing her D.C. power suit and control top pantyhose and the entire time, she'll be talking on her cell phone. Without breaking a sweat, with her perfectly polished finger nails glistening in the sun, she's going to stab that person in the neck with a perfect hostess pickle fork. These Sarah Palin minions don't get up at 04:00 a.m. so some crazy bastard can mess up their commute and throw them off schedule.

The highly intelligent powers that be in the Nation's Capital recognize that the commute in and out of D.C. sucks. The good news is that they have made different commuting options available to help us attack the dreaded commute. The bad news is that none of the options are any good.

The first option is to do the commute into D.C. by car. Coming out of Northern Virginia where I live, Route 66 is the only interstate leading into D.C. Millions of commuters from Northern Virginia spend hours commuting on Route 66, stuck in bumper-to-bumper traffic that is more reminiscent of a parking lot than an interstate. We locals refer to this interstate as Route 666 - *the number of the beast!*

Sixty mph is the posted speed limit, but in the years I've spent riding the brakes down Route 666 I've rarely managed to get my car above thirty-five mph. On days when traffic is really moving and there are no accidents, car fires, children being born in taxis, or hazardous spills, we can drive for miles at the top speed of about 18 mph. On the typical days riding Route 666, traffic will move at 5 mph, then it stops; then it starts moving at 8 mph, then it stops. When I've got the top down on the convertible, I might have to worry about birds settling in and building nests in my backseat, but I'm not even moving fast enough to worry about messing up my hair.

Weekday rush hour on Route 666 heading into D.C. starts at 05:00 a.m. and never ends. Weekday rush hour heading out of D.C. starts at 4:00 p.m. and never ends. The only exception to rush hour times is on Fridays when the rush out of D.C. starts at 12:00 noon and never ends. And if it's a Friday before a long holiday weekend, forget about even trying to get out of D.C. Just rent yourself a hotel room, make yourself comfortable, go see a couple of monuments or visit a museum and try your luck again some other day.

When I first started commuting by car into D.C., I heard all kinds of rumors about something called the commuting window. This rumor still persists and I've even met some people who swear on their dead mother's grave that they've experienced the window in person. According to legend, there is a 15 minute commuting window that opens up at some point right before D.C. rush hour starts. As a result, 4:00 p.m. in D.C. is marked by hundreds of thousands of frantic federal government employees trying to close up shop for the day and get on the road before this window closes. The fairy tale claims that any man fortunate enough to catch the window before it closes will be blessed by the gods above. He will live to see a commute of less than 2 hours, his land will yield him a plentiful crop, and his wife will bear him healthy sons.

I've done the crappy commute down Route 666 for many years and I can tell you that this fabled D.C. commuting window is about as real as unicorns, Sasquatch, or the Chupacabra. The commuting window folklore is nothing but pathetic mythology passed from commuter to commuter.

Within a few months of commuting into D.C. by car, I learned that the secret to surviving the commute on Route 666 was to always have an adequately stocked commuting kit on hand. Although the commuting kit won't lessen the time spent in the commute, it can definitely help make the time a little more bearable.

Starbucks coffee: My coffee of choice is the Venti Caramel Macchiato, ½ skim, ½ soy, sugar-free caramel, extra hot, no foam. The Venti coffee is an excellent choice for the seasoned D.C. commuter who has spent years training, strengthening, and perfecting their bladder control abilities. The novice commuter, however, should under no circumstances attempt any coffee larger than a medium or else they risk putting themselves in danger of an emergency pee situation.

Cell phone, satellite TV, and/or other mobile device: It is imperative to keep communication lines open to the outside world while stuck in traffic on Route 666. Without this communication life line, D.C. commuters can sit trapped for hours in a commuting vacuum, completely oblivious to anything else going on in the world around them. In the time it takes a commuter to drive from Northern Virginia into D.C., Paris Hilton could have a new best friend, Lindsay Lohan could be back in rehab, or Oprah could be skinny again and the pathetic commuter would have sadly missed it all.

<u>Snacks, bottled water, cigarettes, books on tape, meditational CDs, music, prayer</u> The D.C. commuter should ensure access to a variety of entertainment options to help pass the time and keep their mind off the commute, otherwise they risk suffering a complete and total mental break-down.

I had never fully appreciated the legitimacy of road rage until I started commuting by car in and out of D.C. On any given day, it is not uncommon for traffic on Route 666 to get backed-up for 10 mile stretches at a time and when an accident occurs, traffic can back-up the full thirty-mile stretch from VA to the D.C. beltway. And when traffic screws up my commute to that extent, I fully expect - no, I fully *demand* - to drive by the scene of the crash and see someone's brains spattered all over a windshield. At the very least I'd appreciate a glimpse of some miscellaneous body parts littering the freeway or some EMT zipping up a body bag. This way, I know I at least stand a chance of winning the commuting horror story contest when I finally arrive in the office 4 hours later.

As terrible as the commute is on Route 666, there is actually one surprising and positive element to it. The commute into D.C. is so bad it actually gives married couples something other than each other to bitch about. I can tell you with all honesty that my marriage and my bond to my husband has definitely grown stronger during the years I've been forced to commute to and from D.C. by car. Has my relationship grown stronger because I've spent quality hours every day with him enjoying his company and conversation? Perhaps, but mostly I think it's just that I need his body.

Having free and easy access to another living body is imperative to surviving the D.C. commute. A 2nd body in my car when I'm commuting from Northern Virginia heading into D.C. allows me to drive in the special, restricted Route 666 High Occupancy Vehicle (HOV) commuting lanes. HOV lanes are the equivalent of taking the short cut from the kitchen to the conservatory in the Clue board game. During peak rush hour traffic, the HOV lane can literally shave thirty-minutes to an hour off my commute. So, infidelity, credit problems, erectile dysfunction, he's sprouted a 3rd nipple - I don't care. I'll live with it. As long as I'm commuting in and out of Washington, D.C. via Route 666, there is no way in hell I'm divorcing my husband, losing easy access to a body, and giving up my right to drive in the HOV lanes.

After a number of years I decided I could no longer handle driving on Route 666. Every time I got in the car I felt like I wanted to pepper the freeway in gunfire. So as a public service to my fellow commuters, the commuting option I started utilizing was the commuter train, the Virginia Railway Express (VRE). I've been catching the VRE every day for the last 4 years along with the same twelve-hundred other passengers and the most glowing review I can give you about commuting via the VRE is *well, at least it's not Route 666.*

There's absolutely no methodology to predict with any degree of confidence whether or not the VRE will be running on time and on schedule. If it's too cold and the rails might ice over, the

VRE runs slow and behind schedule. If it's raining and the rails might be slippery, the VRE runs slow and behind schedule. If it's windy and leaves have blown onto the track and the rails might be slick, the VRE runs slow and behind schedule. If rumors of a Sasquatch sighting are circulating, the VRE runs slow and behind schedule.

One day the VRE was running behind schedule because the police had to intercept a band of Hobos riding a freight train in front of it. I didn't even know Hobos still existed, but apparently they do. The VRE was stopped for 2 hours as passengers waited on the police to escort 10 adults, 3 kids, and 2 Hobo dogs off the freight train.

There is no en-route movie, and no snacks or drinks are served on the VRE, so you are screwed if you don't think ahead to pack some water and snacks. Last summer I got on board the VRE at 4:30 p.m. and due to some railroad signal and mechanical issues, I didn't make it home until 8:00 p.m. I hadn't had a thing to drink or eat since 11:00 a.m. and I could hear my stomach growling over the VRE engine. In a half exhausted and panicked state of mind, I started to stake a claim on some of the more corpulent passengers who were starting to look like they'd make for some pretty good eating if that's what it was going to come down to. I'm not picking on the obese. All I'm saying is that if it ever came down to cannibalism on the VRE, my preference would be a soft, succulent piece of meat. I like a little fat and gravy on my meat. I can't choke down some dry, stick-thin marathon runner with their 5% body fat and sinewy little chicken legs, especially if I don't have something to wash them down with, is all I'm saying.

On the days when I feel like catching-up on some much needed sleep, I board the VRE's Quiet Car. In concept, the Quiet Car is a great idea – it supposedly provides an environment of silence for commuters who'd like to read, or sleep, or just not be disturbed by idle chit-chat. And the Quiet Car is "quiet" if you don't count the Conductors' booming voices on the overhead speakers every 4 minutes apologizing for running slow and behind schedule.

The most disturbing part about riding in the Quiet Car lately is I've noticed a growing emergence of people I call the Noise Nazis. These Noise Nazis ride the Quiet Cars religiously and they mean business. The Quiet Car rules stipulate that limited whispering is allowed, but otherwise, there is no talking permitted on the Quiet Car. All electronic devices that ring or make other noises must be disabled. Ringers on cell phones must be turned off or the phone must be set to vibrate, and the sound to any electronic games must be muted. If a passenger is listening to music or enjoying a movie via headset or earphones, there is also a Quiet Car rule stipulating that other passengers should not be able to hear the sound coming from the earphones or headset. The Noise Nazis riding the Quiet Cars know these rules. They know the rules, they live the rules, and they enforce the rules. And by *enforce*, I mean they lose their damn minds. Yelling, cell phones physically ripped out of passengers hands, name calling, and shoving are just a few of the altercations I've witnessed in the last 2 years between educated, well employed adults riding in the Quiet Car.

That being said, even though the VRE is slow, runs behind schedule, can be unpredictable, is plagued with Hobos and fanatic Nazis, I think it's still a better commuting option than driving down Route 666.

Slugging is another option available to commuters in the D.C. metro area and it's a commuting practice that is as weird as its name. I don't know what slugs have to do with commuting, or why someone would have thought the term *slugging* would appeal to commuters. If the inventors of slugging asked for my vote, I would have gone with a name that was more realistic and descriptive of the potential risk involved with this form of commuting. Maybe something like *serial killer express.*

I've talked to a number of coworkers who practice slugging and they assure me that it's a completely safe method of commuting and is nothing at all like the dangerous practice of hitch-hiking. With slugging, there are the drivers and there are the people looking to catch a ride, affectionately known as the slugs. The object of slugging is to pair up a driver with a slug headed into the same general area within D.C., allowing the driver to utilize the HOV lanes.

The way slugging works is that a slug will travel to a commuter parking lot that is known for practicing slugging. Once at the parking lot, the slug will wait with other slugs for a driver to pull up and offer him a ride into D.C. The driver only guarantees a ride into D.C. - there is no guaranteed ride out of D.C., so the slug will have to locate another driver when he's ready to leave D.C. It's a short-lived, parasitic relationship.

The slug benefits by getting a free ride into D.C. and the driver benefits by getting to utilize the HOV lanes, thus minimizing his commute. Although slugging still sounds exactly like hitch-hiking to me, I've been told it is absolutely not hitch-hiking. Hitch-hiking is illegal in D.C. We don't hitch-hike in D.C., we *slug*. Understand the difference?

I don't care how you try to coat it, the practice of slugging is nothing more than accepting rides from total strangers and that just goes against everything I've ever been taught. I don't care how long I live in D.C., I can't see myself being comfortable with some random stranger pulling up to me and offering me a ride. Furthermore, accepting rides from total strangers in a city that has repeatedly won the title of "Murder Capital of the USA" just goes against all common sense. But then again, this is Washington, D.C., and there's a lot that happens here that goes against all common sense.

Slugging is so widely practiced in the D.C. Metro area that commuters sometimes forget that outside of D.C., the practice of inviting random strangers into your car is weird and frightening. A few months after moving to D.C., I was standing alone at a bus stop at 5:00 a.m. when a minivan pulled up slowly alongside me and 2 well-dressed, well-groomed men smiled at me from the front seats. They asked where I was headed and wanted to know if I was interested in a ride. I screamed obscenities at them, threw my lunch at their van, screamed for help, and I ran away. I was so shaken up, I didn't even make it to work that morning. It's amazing that more sluggers don't get pepper-sprayed.

But conventional manners don't apply in the Nation's Capital, especially not where the commute is concerned.

Never mind everything your parents have ever taught you about accepting rides from strangers, kids. The next time you're in Washington, D.C. and some bearded stranger in a raincoat and dark glasses offers you a ride, you're supposed to get in his van.

8 NOT MY MOTHER'S TUPPERWARE PARTY

Peer pressure at high school doesn't come close to a suburban housewife's need to host and attend a party. The homes in my Northern Virginia community have recently dropped into the crapper by $200,000 but not even that or the pathetic state of our current economy will prevent parties from being hosted in the suburbs. We literally host a party for every occasion imaginable - welcome to the neighborhood party, a change of season party, my-divorce-is-final party, housewarming party, I'm-redecorating-a-room party, the come-join-us-for-a-drink-and-gossip-about-anyone-who-didn't show-to-this-party party...

Before you even realize what is happening, there are months at a time where your calendar is full and every weekend is spent attending or hosting some kind of party: make up, cooking gadgets, scented candles, costume jewelry - it's never ending. There's a party for absolutely everything and anything that can be ordered over a 1-800 number and will fit into the back of an SUV. These neighborhood parties are what we suburbanites call JUGS (Just Us Girls) events since husbands and kids are neither invited nor welcome.

My indoctrination to the whole party scene came in the form of an innocent enough looking invitation placed in my mailbox within the first few weeks of us moving into our townhouse:

> *Leave the kids at home! Come have a drink & chat with the girls! No pressure to buy anything! *Cash, check, credit cards gladly accepted.*

And so it began.

By accepting that first invitation my name got added to a mass distribution list of participants for all neighborhood JUGS events going forward. I get invitations via email, regular mail, they are slipped under my front door, taped to my back door, and hand-delivered by my son on the occasions he's accosted on his way home from the school bus stop.

In the past I have tried to lie my way out of attending a neighborhood party by claiming some prior commitment, but when you live in a townhouse community like mine, where all the houses stand just a few feet apart from one another, it's virtually impossible not to get caught in the lie. The second one of the neighbors walks by and notices your lights or television set is on, you're caught. Attendance at these parties is absolutely mandatory as is the minimum purchase of $50 worth of product in order for the hostess to qualify for her free gift items.

I'm ashamed to admit that I've even played the sick child card to get me out of attending some parties, but in a small community like mine, you have to completely commit to the lie and be willing to ride it all the way out. Phones immediately start ringing as other concerned moms want to know what affliction the child is suffering from and what the doctor said. *Is he contagious? Does he have a fever? What medicine did the doctor prescribe?* Sometimes it's just easier to show up, shut up, and buy the damn products. So I attend all these parties and it never fails - at least one woman at each of these events will get lured into hosting her own party with the promise of discounted and free gift items as long as she invites at least 6 people and they purchase $50 worth of crap they don't need. And since the only other women she knows are all sitting in the same room with her at the current party... well, you get the picture. It's a never ending merry-go-round.

My very understanding and accepting husband has added another shelf in our living room and another 2 cabinets in our kitchen to accommodate all the scented candles, potpourri, food storage and cooking gadgets I've amassed throughout the years. I think I would actually enjoy using some of the cooking gadgets I've purchased, but I don't have time to cook since I'm always busy attending parties.

My husband and I were sitting in the kitchen one evening sorting through piles of our junk mail (hey, why don't we use some of those smelly candles I bought to set this crap on fire?) when I received the latest party invitation from one of the moms in a neighboring community. After a few minutes of reviewing the catalog that accompanied the invitation, I called one of the other resident moms, Amy, to see if she was planning on attending. She informed me she had already accepted on behalf of both of us.

> "Besides, I need you to be my designated driver because I'm going to have to get stupid drunk to attend this one."

I resignedly agreed to serve as her designated driver *if* and *only if* my husband was ok with me attending this particular kind of party.

> "Hey, honey, I just received an invitation to go with Amy to a party on Saturday evening. You know the drill. Strictly a JUGS event."

> "Ah Jesus, do we really need more Tupperware? Can you please at least try to keep the purchase to about $30-$40 range this time?"

> "Um, well, it's definitely a *rubber product* type party, but it isn't Tupperware ... I guess it's more of a girlie .... um... slumber party

with lotions and intimate apparel and... well here, take a look..."

My Catholic mother would have been proud that I retained enough of my proper Catholic upbringing so that my face flushed with embarrassment as I handed my husband the dildo catalog. "Oh, wow" was my husband's breathless reaction. He let out a low whistle as he slowly flipped through the first few pages of big-boobed models wearing sexy lingerie and high heels. I think he was actually breathing heavier! I don't know why that bothered me so much, but I genuinely wanted to stab him in the throat with my spiked party hostess tomato gripper.

By the time my husband hit the pages in the catalog displaying the wide array of *personal massage* items (batteries not included), he felt compelled to reiterate his concern for the state of our household budget.

"Like I said, can you please try to keep the purchase to about a $300-$400 range this time?"

OK, someone please hand me my spiked party hostess tomato gripper...

Saturday around 7:00 p.m., Amy and I pulled into the driveway of what we thought was the designated house for the dildo party and I instantly thought we were at the wrong place. I don't know what I was expecting, but I was certainly not expecting to see a woman in the driveway wearing a white blouse with a sweater tied around her shoulders. She was a very petite blonde and was wearing a pair of very sensible-looking flat shoes and was busy unloading a vegetable tray from her Volvo SUV.

"Jesus, Amy, we're in the wrong place. Look at her. She's a soccer mom for Chrissakes. They don't do dildos. We're obviously at the wrong address."

As I was throwing my SUV into reverse and starting to back-out of the driveway, out came Allison, the party hostess, running up to greet us and to take the platter from the cute soccer mom. We followed them into the kitchen and adjoining living room where we were formally introduced to the cute blonde, Linda, and a roomful of other seemingly upright, respectable women admiring the buffet. To an outsider looking through the window, we would appear to be a group of decent, God-fearing Republicans attending a church social. The center table displaying the phallic-shaped cake heavily decorated with unruly swirls of black frosting to represent a very generous mass of curly pubic hair would have been the first clue this was no church social.

The dildo party buffet consisted of a large assortment of items I've never seen on any buffet before. There were chocolate candies depicting couples engaged in various sexual acts, with the man and woman bent in all kinds of interesting positions, some of which would land most people in a hospital bed in full-body traction. There was also a variety of boob-shaped gummy candies and hard penis-shaped candies (dick tacs!) to suck on.

"Ok, I'll give you $1 if you put 2 of those boobs in your mouth," Amy snickered as we continued to wander around the room to where the actual party products were on display.

I started to giggle a little nervously as we approached a table holding what appeared to be a long rifle case containing a pretty intimidating piece of hardware.

"Ohmygod! What do you think *that's* used for?"

In all the years I worked in the hospital, I had never seen anything like this particular product. This thing was a huge flesh-colored tubular object. It was about 3-feet long and approximately 6-inches thick and it looked to me like a massive 2-headed mushroom. I certainly would have remembered fishing this out of a patient.

"That's a double-headed dildo. Very popular with the lesbians," Linda informed us nonchalantly as she moved away from us to find a seat.

"Well I'll be damned. I guess soccer moms *do* do dildos!"

I giggled with Amy as we continued to preview the various products that would be for sale after the product demonstrations. Around 8:00 p.m. we were asked to find a seat in the living room where the party was officially about to start.

The party consultant sat us in a large circle and explained that we were going to start off the event with some ice-breakers. The first activity was for each woman to introduce herself by first name only. The challenging part of this introduction was that each woman had to come up with a sex term that started with the same letter as the first letter in her name. The consultant started us off by introducing herself as *Dildo Debbie*. Much nervous laughter and some drunken hilarity erupted as other introductions were made by women at the party - *Lick-it Lisa* and *Panty-sniff Patty*. Amy and I started getting nervous as it got closer to our turns.

"I need your help! I can't think of any word starting with *A* except for *anal*. I don't want to be *Anal Amy*! That is absolutely disgusting!"

"What about me? I can't even think of a sex word that starts with the letter *J*!"

"How about Jism?"

"Jism? Ok, I admit I don't know what that is, but I'm pretty sure I don't do it."

A few seconds later it was my turn to introduce myself to the group of women.

"Um, hi, my name is Janet and well, I'm not really playing ... I'm just here as the designated driver..."

My refusal to play along with the ice breaker resulted in loud booing and hissing from some of the already inebriated ladies, but over the sound of their disapproval, *Jack-Off Janet!* was screamed out loud.

Problem solved. *Jack-Off Janet* it was.

Amy also agreed to the name the group designated for her - *Areola Amy* - and then things started to get interesting.

After all introductions were made, *Dildo Debbie* informed us that the next ice-breaker challenge involved a friend she brought with her named *Big John*. I got scared when I saw that *Big John* was the huge double-headed dildo we were gawking at earlier in the evening. The challenge was for the first woman in the circle to insert *Big John* between her thighs and pass him on to the woman sitting next to her. The object of the game was to pass him around the room from woman to woman without dropping him. We could use any part of our bodies to grab and pass him along to the next person, but we could not use our hands.

The first 2 women positioned themselves facing each other, boob-to-boob, with *Big John* inserted between their thighs to begin the challenge. It became immediately obvious that *Big John*, though most certainly big, was also most certainly *flaccid*. Hysterics ensued as several women pulled out cameras to capture the very creative maneuvers women were employing as they were determined to pass *Big John* on his way around the room without dropping him or spilling their drinks.

Big John made his rounds wedged between women's thighs, their knees, nestled under their chins, and one very well-endowed woman even managed to secure him in her cleavage before passing him on to the next woman. Women were straddling the thighs of other women, bumping and grinding up against each other, and laughing hysterically as they attempted to dislodge *Big John* from wherever he resided on their body and pass him along.

I am still keeping a very nervous watch on the Internet, dreading the materialization of these photos for the entire world and my mother to see.

As the night progressed more drinks were poured and the party started getting very loud and very silly. *Dildo Debbie* would showcase a specific sex-aid item and then she would pass it around the room so that each woman could get a closer look, touch it, taste it, or sniff it, whichever was appropriate to that particular item. Lotions, glitters, dildos, edible underwear, butt plugs, nipple rings, oils, bondage items... you name it, we held it, sniffed it, and tried it on for size. And it's all good and fun until someone loses an eye or inserts something in a bodily orifice for which it was not intended.

Now I know that I agreed to be *Areola Amy's* designated driver at this party, and as such, I was strictly sticking to drinking water and diet cokes all night. I understood that my job was to ensure that she made it home to her husband and family safely. I did not appreciate, however, that my job would also entail making sure she made it through the sampling of sex paraphernalia safely. Amy was apparently becoming heavily inebriated rather quickly and, as I was a little distracted by everything going on around me, I admit I wasn't exactly doing a great job at keeping track of how much she was drinking. In fact, I didn't notice she was starting to have trouble distinguishing between the various party products that were being passed around the circle.

So where was *Jack-Off Janet* when her friend needed her the most? What could I have been doing that would take me away from my very important job of looking out for my friend's safety? Well, I was a little preoccupied with my own traumatic event, thankyouverymuch, and apparently no one at that party was looking out for me or my nipples. While Amy was doing her sex-aid sampling, I found myself involved in one very awkward situation involving my breasts and some faux clip-on nipple rings. So awkward, in fact, it was hard to force myself to call out for help – at least it was hard for the first 20 seconds or so, and then I found it quite easy to scream out for assistance.

I thought it would be hilarious to surprise my husband with some fake nipple rings, and they were only something like $10, so I thought why not? I walked into the bathroom and proceeded to try a pair on for size. The clip-on nipple rings were very easy to apply, just like the consultant promised, and initially they didn't hurt. Within a handful of seconds, however, I became desperate to free myself from the painful grasp of the clips.

I can't even come up with a word that adequately describes the hot, stabbing pain that shot from my breasts. I could literally feel the blood supply being choked out of my nipples and I was scared if I didn't remove them immediately, I would completely and permanently lose all feeling. So that's what I was preoccupied with and why I didn't realize Amy was in trouble until it was too late.

"Duzzz yer tongue feel awwwl numm and funny?" Amy asked me as I returned to the party circle holding plastic sandwich bags filled with ice chips pressed against my boobs.

Amy turned to stick out her tongue so I could examine her mouth that was for reasons unknown to me, heavily sprinkled with green and blue glitter.

"OhSweetMotherofJesus!" I shrieked when I looked down at her hand which was holding a half-empty tube of Anal Ease numbing gel.

Fear gripped me and I dropped my ice packs as I grabbed the tube away from her. In her inebriated state, Amy apparently had consumed what appeared to be a sizeable portion of this product. In case you're not familiar, Anal Ease numbing gel is meant to do *exactly* what the name sounds like it would do. No warning label needed here, folks. I had a feeling that this product was probably not considered safe to be taken orally in any quantity. I couldn't believe she managed to choke down any of that gel. There's no way a product called Anal Ease could possibly contain any palatable ingredients or would have any culinary appeal whatsoever - unless of course it was being sampled by a person who was extremely drunk and their mouth was heavily sprinkled with green and blue glitter.

I grabbed Amy by the wrists and *Dildo Debbie* and I half-dragged her to the kitchen sink so we could flush out her mouth with cold water. After a few minutes the water appeared to be doing the trick and Amy started to slowly regain feeling to her tongue and mouth.

"I still don't want to be called Anal Amy!"

"Yeah, I think she's going to be just fine."

I helped get Amy settled back in the party circle as the consultant assured me that the remainder of the Anal Ease would eventually work its way out of her body. And by *eventually* she apparently meant it would work its way out of Amy's body 20 minutes into our car ride home when she projectile vomited all over my passenger seat, door, and window.

After I dropped Amy off at her house, I returned home to my husband at 2:00 a.m., looking and smelling like a cheap hooker. My clothes were disheveled and dusted with glitter. I had gel and glitter stuck in my hair. I reeked of different lotions, massage oils, and vomit. My nipples were throbbing and I was limping – I'm not exactly sure why. I was exhausted and I was carrying my bra in my purse.

My husband was still awake and was sitting on the couch when I limped in. I tossed the little bag of party product I purchased into his lap and I left him alone with the TV.

"Go for it. Have fun. I am going to disinfect my body and then I'm going to bed. Alone. To sleep."

Because I was invited to the party, I felt obligated to purchase at least one item so the party hostess could get her discounts and free products. To my husband's disappointment, I opted to be fiscally conservative and did not spend the $300-$400 he had budgeted for me. Instead, I purchased a sensible and affordable product, the $22 Coochie Cream shaving and moisturizing lotion gift set.

Coochie Cream, for those of you not current on your coochie products, is a lotion that moisturizes without feeling greasy. It is purportedly used by women when they shave their um...*coochies.* According to the manufacturer, Coochie Cream prevents rashes, ingrown hairs, razor burn, and comes highly recommended by professionals.

I have never seen any pharmaceutical studies or read any scientific testimonials concerning Coochie Cream, so I'm not sure what kind of *professionals* were sought for their reviews. I can tell you, however, that I love the way it smells and I love the silkiness of this product.

Although I can't tell you how effective Coochie Cream works for its intended purpose, I can tell you that since I've started using it, my armpits have never felt smoother.

Made in the USA
Lexington, KY
12 November 2014